MARTIAL
A Social Guide

Art L. Spisak

Duckworth

141384914

2-13-08

First published in 2007 by
Gerald Duckworth & Co. Ltd.
90-93 Cowcross Street, London EC1M 6BF
Tel: 020 7490 7300
Fax: 020 7490 0080
inquiries@duckworth-publishers.co.uk
www.ducknet.co.uk

A catalogue record for this book is available
from the British Library

ISBN-10: 0 7156 36200
ISBN-13: 97807156 36206

Typeset by Ray Davies
Printed and bound in Great Britain by
MPG Books Limited, Bodmin, Cornwall

Contents

Introduction

... the picture [of Martial] presented in our literary histories is that of a fundamentally incoherent poet, obsessed with his personal situation, at the mercy of random sexual and social prejudices; an opportunistic poet with a commonplace philosophy, who has chosen the *minor* genre of epigram to display his skills at light verse, to be rated as inferior even in this to his acknowledged model Catullus ...[1]

The problem

Martial's poetry has survived for almost two millennia and over that long span of time has entertained many readers with its wit while also enlightening them with its perceptive treatment of human behaviour. Yet, as entertaining and engaging as people have found Martial's poetry, because of the particular literary and social milieu that has influenced and shaped its form, content, and tone, it has been much misunderstood and maligned. Most frequently it has been slighted as poetry not worth much consideration: compare, for example, John Sullivan's summarization (above) of the particular objections which critics and general readers have had to it in the past.[2] Then, in reaction to such devaluation of Martial's poetry, some scholarship in the recent past has swung to the other extreme: over-interpretation of the text, for example, attributing a politically subversive subtext to it.[3] Much of this slighting, maligning, and over-interpretation of Martial's poetry can be remedied by an understanding of how it fits into the literary tradition and also its social context: specifically, how Martial's poetry related to the iambic tradition in ancient Greek literature, and then to Catullus' poetry and Roman satire; and also how his poetry reflected and took meaning from the social practices of his readership.

As a good representative example of the maligning of his work, one could consider the criticism of the obscenity and sexual content in

1

Martial's poetry, which in the main has led to damning misperceptions about the significance of his verse. The 1919 Loeb English translation of the poems of Martial by Walter C.A. Ker had the so-called 'indescribably foul' epigrams rendered into Italian.[4] Certainly Ker should be given much credit for even doing a translation of Martial at all – a daring undertaking at that time – and for his rendering into English of at least some of the so-called 'objectionable' poems, albeit with obscenities either deleted or very loosely and benignly paraphrased. Ker's only explanation of his censoring of Martial's poems' obscenity and sexual content was: 'All epigrams possible of translation by use of dashes or paraphrases have been rendered into English, the wholly impossible ones only in Italian.'[5] As it turns out, this obscenity and sexual material is very important to Martial's poetry – that is, there is good reason for his use of it.[6] For, as Martial himself indicates, obscenity and sexual content were a vital part of his poetry: they were, in fact, as will be shown, part of his unique way of reaching his audience.[7] Particularly damaging is the impression that such doctoring and rendering of the Latin text gives of Martial: as if he were only some smut peddler with little literary and personal integrity.

Other elements of Martial's poetry – such as its alleged preoccupation with money or adulation of the Emperor Domitian, who is generally perceived as bad – have produced similarly misguided reactions. Just a few quotations as examples will suffice. Martial has been perceived as an 'unlovely character who courted the favours of the great with the grossest flattery'.[8] Yet, in fact, behind Martial's alleged preoccupation with money and his seemingly excessive praise of friends and emperor is a sophisticated system of social exchange or reciprocity that was fundamental to friendship, business, politics, and sense of community in the ancient Roman world (and remains so today). Also Martial has been described as 'a court jester' who 'never makes us think' and whose poetry is 'unobjectionably trivial' and without any 'moral reflection'.[9] Court jester can indeed apply to Martial, but only if one is aware of the serious and vital role jesters traditionally were expected to fulfil for society: namely, to speak the truth candidly, although never maliciously, to those who most need to hear it, but oftentimes do not – that is, powerful persons. As for the charge that Martial's poetry never makes us think and is trivial and without moral reflection, that perhaps results from the festive, play-

2

ful, and humorous tone that Martial employs: something that makes the truth more palatable to his audience. In fact, his verse, although certainly not intellectually deep or profound, is highly inspirited, affective, and ethical in tone: that is, it affects the emotions and the spirit, and always reflects ancient Roman social views and practices.

To make matters even more confusing, Martial (via his poet-persona) more than a few times claims that his poetry is written for entertainment and fun.[10] Indeed, he rejects the laborious process of writing what was traditionally considered to be serious and worthwhile poetry, namely epic or tragedy, in order to write his own brand of so-called light poetry (see, e.g., epigram 8.3.11-22). At the same time, though, Martial claims that his poetry is actually of more value than poetry of the so-called higher genres, epic and tragedy, for example, because it is about real-life issues and actually has something useful and beneficial to say to its reader (see, e.g., 4.49). Moreover, his poetry is very well crafted, frequently allusive and referential, thus showing his familiarity and facility with the Greek and Roman literary tradition, all of which suggests that he did take his role as a poet very seriously. As a result, even critics with the best intentions sometimes hardly know what to make of his poetry: for it turns out that his poems are as easy to over-interpret as they are to dismiss as hardly worth consideration.[11]

In response to this ambiguity of the nature and effect of Martial's poetry, this study, through consideration of Martial's connection with the literary tradition and the social context for his poetry, addresses this general question: how did his poems affect his audience. Of primary concern here, besides the already mentioned objections to certain areas of content of Martial's poetry (for example sexual material or adulation), is whether Martial's poetry had the effect of being anything more than entertaining. This study maintains that Martial certainly entertained with his poems, but that they, in the main, were also meant to instruct at a personal level.[12] The aggregate result of this instruction at the personal level was a manual or guide that reflected and voiced the ethical views and concerns of his readership. As Sullivan puts it:

> In fact almost all of Martial's work is focused by a unified and hierarchical vision of imperial society as it should be ... It is a

vision coloured by a very personal view of how life should be lived
and the Epicurean values it should manifest, a life that is shel-
tered in the bosom of generous friends with a modest competence
secured by a warm acceptance of the ideological status quo.[13]

The resulting effect of that guide, in turn, was the unifying and
strengthening of the social group through the expression of its views.

Happily, Martial's poetry in the last several decades has found a
more open-minded and objective reception and treatment than in
previous times, thus making this study's goals easier to reach.
Groundbreaking work was done by Niklas Holzberg with his earlier
work on Martial: first an article that presented a new assessment of
Martial's work (1986), and then an introductory book on Martial
(1988), which helped to return respectability to what had been a *dé
classé* poet. Next was J.P. Sullivan's monograph on Martial (1991):
Sullivan, like Holzberg, did much to re-establish Martial's reputation
as a poet in the face of some deeply entrenched prejudice.[14] The latest
Loeb translation of Martial's epigrams by D.R. Shackleton Bailey, in
which all the epigrams are translated into English, almost always
replete with the original obscenities and with helpful explanatory
notes, gives the reader a better feel for the sense of the poetry.[15] There
is also now for the first time a collection of essays, edited by Farouk
Grewing, solely on Martial; there are, as well, more than a few
excellent commentaries, with more appearing, on individual books
that are most helpful for understanding and appreciating Martial's
poetry in the context of his literary, historical, political, and social
milieu.[16] Likewise there has been a stream of worthwhile articles on
various aspects of Martial's poetry (many of which are referenced
below), and also several additional scholarly and provocative book-
length studies on Martial.[17] This recent scholarship does much better
justice to the sophistication and significance of Martial's poetry within
its literary and social context, and this study builds on these works.[18]

The ancient Greek iambic tradition

In response to the question of the significance and effect of Martial's
poetry, this study compares Martial's main corpus – that is, the
twelve-book collection – to the ancient Greek literary tradition of

iambics. The roots of the iambic tradition are somewhat hazy. It appears to have as its precursor the very old Indo-European tradition of blame/praise poetry.[19] In the Indo-European tradition the poet-singer functioned as a specially gifted spokesperson of the social community in doling out both blame and praise to members of the social group. The Indo-European poet-singer was best known, however, for satirical songs that accused persons of grievous character faults. As Ward puts it:

> Greek, Celtic, Germanic and Vedic poetry contains many examples of satirical songs which accuse the victim of grievous character faults. IE [Indo-European] social behavior was motivated more by a sense of public reputation than by the concept of private guilt. Such songs, lampooning instances of greed, inhospitality, breach of promise and moral perversion, consequently served as a powerful form of social control.[20]

The poet-singers of this tradition were so powerful and influential, so respected and feared, that their songs were perceived as having a magical or supernatural effect.[21] At least some of this power and mystique of the Indo-European tradition of invective verse carried over to the ancient Greek iambic tradition, and then down to through ancient Greek Old Comedy to Roman satire and epigram: specifically, the iambic poet always had special licence and a religious and social sanction for his oftentimes scurrilous and direct treatment of aberrant social behaviour in the community; also his power was respected and feared.[22]

Aside from the ancient Greek iambic tradition's similarity to Indo-European blame poetry, its exact nature is somewhat hazy. Although ἴαμβος is a metrical term, that sense is secondary, for in origin it included poems of a variety of metre, subject, and tone.[23] Indeed, the genre is so amorphous that Nagy, in his foreword to a collection of essays on the iambic form or 'idea', comments:

> What emerges most clearly from these studies is that the 'iambic idea' is impossible to define in absolute terms: rather the form ... of iambic keeps on varying in response to a vast variety of historical contingencies... In the end, what is most characteristic about the 'iambic' is its inherent variability ...[24]

Invective, however, is certainly its outstanding feature: as Gerber puts it, ' "Scornful abuse," "bitter tone," and (sexual) "license": these are terms frequently used to describe iambus in general and in particular the poetry of Archilochus and Hipponax.'[25]

Besides the component of invective, there is another common characteristic of iambi: Dover, seconded by West, has suggested that this might be the type of occasion for which they were composed – their 'social context', which was at least originally festive and related to the divinities Demeter or Dionysus.[26] The genre never loses this festive social or communal aspect: it is always meant for some public or social occasion – a symposium, for example – and always caters to a particular social group with the purpose of reaffirming the unity of that group.[27] As Mankin describes the social or communal nature of iambic verse:

> The sense of what was appropriate or dangerous was provided not so much by the individual iambist's sensibilities as by the norms of his society. *Iambus* was composed primarily for an audience drawn from that society, whether the citizens in the assembly, or smaller groups in the predominant social context of archaic Greece, the symposium. In either circumstance, the *iambus* was meant to remind the audience of what might be a threat to the very shared customs, morals, and so on which brought them together and united them as an audience. Whether as fellow citizens or as drinking companions, the members would consider themselves *philoi* ('friends') and what they shared as *philotes* ('friendship'), a term which has the same complex range of meaning in Greek as *amicitia* has in Latin ...[28]

As for a particular definition of the nature of iambic verse, West makes the following observations about Ionian iambus:

> It is always a poetic monologue, or a monody of simple structure. Conversations appear in it, but sometimes it is clear that they are reported by a narrator ... The characteristic metres are iambic trimeter and trochaic tetrameter, either pure or scazon, or epodic combinations. The speaker sometimes addresses himself to the public ... sometimes to an individual, who may be a friend ... but is more often the subject of mockery or worse ... He

6

ridicules or denounces particular persons or universal types, in an amusing or entertaining way, or he tells tales of titillating sexual adventures or other low doings. He may represent himself as something of a clown, he may assume a different character altogether, at least at the beginning of the performance.

1974, 32

As for content, West notes the following about Archilochus and the other ancient Greek iambic poets: they have written on, or in honour of, the divinities Demeter, Kore, and Dionysus; they wrote invective, which can include explicitly sexual and vulgar content as well as attacks on women; they employed a burlesque admixture of the high-flown (West uses the *Margites* – ascribed to Homer – as an example); they made many references to food and foodstuffs; and finally, they wrote poems that may be termed philosophic (West gives Semonides 1 as an example: a sermon on the vanity of human aspirations and the uselessness of worrying: 1974, 23-32).

Such are the general nature and characteristics of ancient Greek iambic poetry as formulated by West and other scholars. Although invective was a distinctive feature of it, the iambic mode was more than poetry with an abusive tone. Its metre and subject-matter varied, as did its format and tone. The two common characteristics of iambi, however, are invective and the type of occasion for which they were composed, their social context, which was at least originally festive and communal: they were always meant for some public or social occasion and always reflected that particular social group's ethic, with the purpose of reaffirming the unity of that group. In that respect, as well as with the component of invective, the Indo-European tradition of blame/praise poetry, which functioned as a form of social control, appears to have been a precursor of the iambic tradition.

Martial as iambographer

Martial's epigrams share many common elements with ancient Greek iambi. Obviously his poetry's strong invective component (see next chapter) connects him with the iambic tradition, as does his poetry's pronounced social context. For Martial's poems do indeed have a strong social context to them in that they are both festive and communal in their tone and content. Some of the books, for example, were probably written for release for the Roman festival of Saturnalia and reflect the celebratory atmosphere typical of that major, religiously based holiday.[29] Yet all the books, whether written for release for a holiday or not, have a festive quality to them in that they are meant to entertain: over and over Martial tells his reader that his poems, or his jokes, as he sometimes terms them, are meant for the evening hours when the reader has been relaxed by food, drink, and conviviality.[30] Also, Martial's poetry is a personal commentary on the situations and social practices of his readership, and hence is communal in that it is a record or catalogue of the social views shared by that group. A bit of Roman literary history on the epigram will confirm this last claim.

The earliest literary Latin epigrams – as opposed to strictly inscriptional epigrams (sepulchral, commemorative, or dedicatory inscriptions) – that have survived date from the end of the second and the beginning of the first centuries BCE.[31] These poems, by various authors, share characteristics with Martial's brand of epigram – brevity, polish, playfulness, select metres – but are also highly varied in form, content, and tone.[32] What all these early epigrams seem to have in common, however, is that they were written by upper class Romans in their leisure time for circulation among their friends.[33] This type of verse – what may be termed *vers de société* or social verse – which was written by members of the Roman nobility, who then shared it with their friends, was taken up and developed by Catullus and the neoterics, the new poets.[34] As Citroni describes it (1996, 537):

> This production of everyday minor verse at Rome, the product of leisure and an ingredient in social relations, increased in the time of Caesar and Augustus... It was an important element in the work of Catullus and the other 'new poets', who wrote short poems to accompany gifts, to console or thank, invite or congratulate, to celebrate (seriously or humorously) the most diverse events of the society in which they lived, and to engage in polemic and invective on public and private matters.

After noting various collections of epigrams (or *poemata*, 'poems', or otherwise designated) attributed to these new poets, Citroni then says in description of this new literary movement:

8

The verses of these poets, with those of Catullus, signal the birth of a new literary language for the description of everyday life, at times delicate, at times realistic and incisive, even crude and obscene, but always artistically light and elegant. The Catullan or neoteric 'revolution' was the use of this genre and language to express an intensely personal emotional world and to affirm the system of values in which even the smallest day-to-day event, rather than being the subject of amateur versifying, became the occasion for poetry of the highest level which could absorb all the energies of a poet of the greatest ambition.

Citroni's comments reveal the many elements this Roman *vers de société* had in common with ancient Greek iambi: frequently a mocking or derisive tone; a conversational and personal style, sometimes including obscenity; a variety in subject-matter; and, most striking, a social or communal context. For epigram certainly was communal in that through the poet's description of, and reaction to, everyday events it directly reflected the concerns, feelings, and values of the poet's audience. These many shared components and especially the social component of Roman epigram suggest that Catullus was much influenced by the iambic tradition.

The strong influence of the iambic tradition on Catullus has recently been argued by J.K. Newman, who goes so far as to categorize Catullus as an iambographer *cum* Roman satirist, rather than a love-poet or lyricist.[35] In brief, Newman posits that Catullus' poetry was descended from ancient Greek iambic poetry, as first practised by Archilochus. Archilochus' ἰαμβικὴ ἰδέα, 'iambic mode' (or 'form'), Newman argues, was much broader than has traditionally been perceived: although invective poetry was its main characteristic, it also included poems in a variety of styles and tones.[36] In defining his extended conception of the iambic tradition Newman draws upon a list drawn up by Dover of seven characteristics of preliterate song, upon which, Dover posits, iambic poets drew for their material, style, and tone.[37] Briefly, as formulated by Dover, preliterate songs had in general the following characteristics:

(1) They commonly expressed an emotional reaction to an event that was usually treated as happening at present and was most commonly actual.

9

(2) They were addressed to a person or category of person whom the poet would have occasion to address in ordinary life.
(3) The emotion they expressed was not necessarily that of the composer.
(4) They often included sexual material.
(5) They included animal fables.

All except the last are indeed characteristic of Catullus' poetry.

This complex and extended form of the iambic mode, Newman maintains, was first instituted in the Roman literary tradition by the satirist Lucilius, and then was taken up by Catullus, who tried to give Lucilius' unsophisticated or rough style a more acceptable literary form by adopting Alexandrian technique. The specific features of Newman's extended conception of Archilochus' ἰαμβικὴ ἰδέα as applied to Catullus' poetry are: public blaming (*vituperatio*); parody of the heroic world; 'flyting' between the sexes; the dialogue format; 'φίλος language', the language of love and/or friendship as developed by Catullus into a 'doctrine of *amor/amicitia*'; the theme of the 'grotesque body' or *deformitas*, to use the Latin term; the use of *inversa verba* (*double entendre*), words that have more than one sense and hence give the poem a metaphorical sense; irony; the speaker mocking himself; and, finally, obscenity (1990, 58-9). Again, although one might not go so far as to classify Catullus as an iambographer, certainly Newman's argument indicates the strong influence the iambic tradition seems to have had on Catullus.

Catullus is especially important in this brief literary history of epigram because Martial specifically names him as his model.[38] This may be surprising at first glance because of the great variety of poems we have from Catullus, some of which defy exact classification. Yet the many poems that are obviously epigrammatic in form and style (especially *cc.* 69-116, but also at least some of the *polymetra*) make him, with the exception of his *epyllion*, an understandable choice as Martial's model.[39] Certainly the majority of Catullus' poems from *c.* 69 to 116 have the characteristics of epigram: they tend to be occasional (written for a specific instance), sometimes rhetorically pointed in style, sometimes invective in tone, sometimes with obscenity or risqué content, and all written in elegiac metre.[40] The strongest link between Martial and Catullus, however, runs deeper: both poets were writing *vers de société*, conversational and personal comments on everyday life that presented and reflected the social practices and values of their audience. As Sullivan phrases it, that which was most unique about Catullus' poetry and what Martial may have found most attractive was 'the strong personal element that Catullus introduced into the epigram tradition, the willingness to talk about himself, his sex life, his emotional reactions, his friends and social activities.'[41]

Although Martial's poems do not have the same emotional intensity (sentimentality and eroticism) and personal individuality as do Catullus', they nonetheless speak of personal and social matters in a forthright manner, and thus mirror the social views, the ethics, of his audience. The remarks of Pliny, Martial's contemporary, on his own poetry show the social aspect of epigram in general: Pliny begins one of his letters by saying that he is not sending, as usual, an *oratio*, 'speech', but rather some of his *lusus*, 'playthings', as he terms his poems. He continues:

> You will receive with this letter my hendecasyllables, with which I amuse myself during the time I have while in my carriage, the bath, or at dinner. With these we jest, play, love, express sorrow, complain, and express anger; sometimes we use a plain style, sometimes more elevated, and I try through variety itself to make it so that certain things may please everyone.
>
> *Ep.* 4.14.2-4

Then, near the end of this letter, Pliny says that he intends to give his *nugae*, 'trifles', the title of 'hendecasyllables', but that they also could be called 'epigrams, idylls, eclogues, or simply "short poems" [*poematia*], which is the popular name' (4.14.8-10). Similarly, in another letter Pliny makes this recommendation to his addressee on what course of study to follow during a long holiday:

> It is permitted, also, to be refreshed by (writing) poetry – I don't mean by an extended and long poem (that which it is not possible to finish unless at leisure), but with the kind that is polished and short, which can break up your occupations and concerns, however many they are. These are called playthings [*lusus*], but

these playthings sometimes bring no less fame than serious work... They [i.e. these short poems] have to do with what we love, hate, our anger, compassion, and wit – in short, everything that occupies us in life and also in the forum and in court.

Ep. 7.9.8-14

In effect, Pliny has defined Latin epigram for his own time – late first century CE – but the description also fits Catullus' poetry because of the personal view it presents of social practices and views. Thus, the deeper connection between Martial and Catullus was that they were both writing *vers de société* – verse written specifically to be the voice of their audience in that it reflected the thoughts and feelings of that audience about everyday matters.

Martial's poetry, then, as well as Catullus' shows the strong influence of the iambic tradition through its format of *vers de société*.[42] Both poets wrote verse for social occasions, but also poems about everyday social events and human behaviour. Their poetry, therefore, was communal in the sense that it was a personal commentary on the social practices of their audience, as was the ancient Greek iambus. In addition, both poets show the influence of the iambic tradition with their invective and use of obscenity, the other common and distinguishing component of iambi. Martial, however, because so very many of the poems of his main corpus are centred on everyday events and social behaviour, often employing abusive and obscene language and imagery, seems to rate the title of iambographer even more than Catullus. Support for his role as an iambographer will be further detailed in the following chapters.

If he is considered as working in the iambic tradition, the significance and effect of Martial's poetry become clearer. His poetry could be described as a social guide in both its senses. First, his poetry reflected and in effect was a catalogue of the social practices and views of his audience: it was a record of social practices. Secondly, Martial was a social guide in that his poetry illustrated and thus encouraged proper behaviour to his reader at a personal level. Specifically, in reaction to any perceived deterioration of the behaviour and conditions of his day he ridiculed socially aberrant and dangerously destructive conduct; or, less often, in an effort to prescribe and encourage socially acceptable conduct, he praised examples of ideal behaviour. This praise and ridicule had the effect of reaffirming and strengthening the traditional structure of society. Thus, Martial, as did the iambic poet, served a vital function for his audience and society. His role as an iambic poet will be further detailed in the following chapters.

1

Invective

Blessed is he who is praised; woe to him who is satirized, Aed.[1]

The influence and power of Indo-European poet-singers is legendary.[2] Indeed, their power was such that in the sixth century CE even the Irish King Aed, addressed in warning by St Columba in the above quotation, feared them so much that he sought to eliminate altogether the profession of poet-singers.[3] No one, no matter how highly placed or powerful, was beyond their reach. Martial, in the spirit of this Indo-European tradition, likewise made much use of the weapon of blame and ridicule – indeed, satire or invective was his most prevalent component in the twelve-book collection.[4] This chapter examines the tradition behind Martial's invective, which he himself often characterizes as his *ioci*, his 'jokes' or 'jests'.[5] This literary tradition of invective suggests that the effect of Martial's abusive jokes, which were oftentimes obscene and sexually graphic, was to bring his reader to recognize, celebrate, and reconnect with the basic human feelings, drives, and instincts. Of course any changes Martial's poetry might bring about in an individual's behaviour, character, and well-being would have a direct bearing on the health of the social community. It is thus argued that Martial's invective did help his social community to achieve and maintain a unified, healthy, and productive state.

The origin of Greek iambics

The strong component of invective in Indo-European blame poetry has been discussed briefly in the previous chapter. Also covered was the related tradition of ancient Greek iambic poetry, which had invective as one of its two most distinguishing features. The story of the origin of iambic poetry in ancient Greek myth helps reveal the workings and intended effect of its obscene, invective component.[6] Iambics are said to have originated in the words and actions of the character of Iambe (the eponym of the iambic metre) as related in the Homeric *Hymn to Demeter*. The story is that Demeter, in deep mourning over the kidnapping of her daughter, had left Olympus and her duties as agricultural goddess to come down to Eleusis as an old woman; there she had been persuaded to enter the house of Queen Metaneira and King Celeus. At first, she, because of her deep grief over the loss of her daughter, refused to accept anything from her hostess – neither a seat, nor food, nor drink (192-201). She even abstained from any word or gesture (199), all of which behaviour was certainly abnormal and even insulting to her hostess, who had offered her hospitality. This deep, antisocial spell of grief was finally broken by Iambe, one of the attendants of the royal house in the following way:

> Unsmiling, tasting neither food nor drink, she [Demeter] sat wasting with desire for her deep-girt daughter, until knowing Iambe jested [χλεύης] with her and mocking with many a joke [πολλὰ παρασκώπτουσ'] moved the holy goddess to smile and laugh and keep a gracious heart – Iambe, who even afterward continued to please her in her rites.
>
> *Hymn to Demeter* 200-5

Iambe manages to break Demeter from her deep-seated grief through her mocking jokes. Moreover, although Iambe's exact remarks are not made explicit here, the words used for the joking and comments on the passage by ancient authors indicate that her jokes were the mythical prototype of a ritual abuse (αἰσχρολογία) that was part of the Eleusinian ritual: these jokes were comic, abusive, and, by all indications, obscene.[7] Indeed, in the Orphic version of the story, as Clement describes the event, Baubo, a counterpart to Iambe, goes even further in her efforts to dispel Demeter's grief.[8] At first Baubo tries to induce Demeter with words to accept the hospitality of the house. Then, unable to reach Demeter in that manner, she tries something else:

> Having spoken thus, she [Baubo] lifted up her dress and showed all the indecent parts of her body. And the child Iacchus was there, and, laughing, was putting his hand under Baubo's breast. And so then the goddess laughed – laughed in her heart – and received the shining cup, in which the malt was held.[9]

16

1. Invective

The specific purpose of Iambe's mocking and obscene jokes in the *Hymn* and the ostentatious sexual display in the Baubo version clearly were to jolt Demeter from her antisocial and unnatural condition – a condition not only insulting to Iambe's mistress, but also dangerous to mortals, as it turns out, because Demeter, in her grief over the loss of her daughter, had left off her duties as agricultural goddess, which made famine inevitable. Since Demeter had not responded to the normal means of initiating the bond of friendship (the offer of food, drink, and conversation), Iambe, in a reversal or inversion of the normal, instead mocks and uses obscenity (or lewd display, in the case of Baubo) in order to reach her. This obscenity and the sexual nature of Iambe's jokes and Baubo's display seem especially appropriate in helping Demeter to reconnect to her role as fertility goddess:[10] as if Baubo, who herself is sometimes depicted as the personification of the female genital organs, with her display of her genitals was recalling Demeter to that aspect of herself.[11] Also, the introduction into the Baubo version of the story of the character Iacchus – Bacchus or Dionysus, a male fertility god who is seen as Demeter's counterpart – reinforces the idea of release through earthy humour or obscene jest, again with the associations of obscenity and fertility. In short, Iambe (or Baubo) induces laughter through her mocking and obscene jokes in order to recall Demeter from her deadening grief: thus does she effect a rebirth in the goddess.[12]

Iambe's use of obscene and abusive humour with Demeter, then, reveals the root purpose of the practice, a cause that seems to underlie its use in invective. She used such extreme measures in order to reach and redress a social infraction – Demeter's refusal of hospitality – that had responded to none of the normal means of treatment. This extreme treatment was meant to reconnect Demeter to the normal order of things and thus restore health to her and, as it turns out in this myth, ultimately to the social community. As Brown conjectures, Iambe's obscene and abusive taunts are in reaction to the 'cosmic crisis' caused by Demeter's mourning for her daughter – that is, crops fail to grow and the human race faces extinction; Iambe's taunts, an inversion of normal behaviour, are in reaction to Demeter's inverted behaviour, and have as their purpose the reaffirmation and strengthening of 'the traditional structures of society and even the natural world'.[13] Thus, the devices of wit, humour, and laughter produced by

17

the obscenity and sexual content are tools not for a malicious attack against Demeter – for that itself would have been a violation of hospitality. Rather, they are meant through their unconventional and shockingly base humour to move the goddess from her antisocial and unnatural state of mind, and bring her back to her social self and eventually to her communal function as mother and goddess of agriculture.

These mocking and obscene jokes that Iambe used on Demeter become a regular feature of the festivals of Demeter – part of the ritual of her cult;[14] and from the cultic practice came, in turn, the literary practice, via Archilochus, the first of Greek iambic poets.[15] Several things tie Archilochus to these ritualized, obscene jokes. First, he was born and lived on Paros (an island in the Cyclades), which was the home of an important cult, both for Demeter and for Baubo, Iambe's counterpart.[16] Secondly, his family was thought to be involved in the cult worship of Demeter.[17] Thirdly, Archilochus had his poetry performed at religious festivals.[18] Additional proof of Archilochus' iambic verse being publicly performed, although it involves the god Dionysus rather than Demeter, is the story that at a certain festival Archilochus had once improvised some verses and taught them to a chorus:[19] these verses made mention of Dionysus and Oipholios, 'the Screwer', which was probably an epithet or title of Dionysus, as well as mentioning grapes and figs, probably with sexual *double entendre*. The city found the verses objectionable because they were 'too iambic' (ἰαμβικώτερον) – presumably because of their suggestive or obscene language, and Archilochus was put on trial for composing them.[20] The men of the city, however, were soon after struck with impotence. They sent to Delphi to find the remedy and were told they must honour Archilochus, servant of the Muses, before harsh Bacchus could be appeased. All this suggests that Archilochus took part in the abusive and obscene taunts, the αἰσχρολογία, that were part of Demeter's rituals as well as those of Dionysus, and created poems from the inspiration he received from them, thus initiating 'literary iambus'.[21] The roots of the literary iambic form, then, seem to have been initiated by Archilochus through his association with the rituals of Demeter and Dionysus.

The iambic form was taken up by Simonides and Hipponax, the other Greek iambic poets, and then by the writers of New Comedy.[22] Characteristic of the form throughout were the mocking and obscene jokes, sometimes used in attacks on individuals, sometimes on groups.[23] Yet, the communal and ritualistic roots and the social context of these mocking jokes – as evident in the *Hymn to Demeter* – took them beyond personal attacks. A good illustration of how the invective component of iambic poetry transcended the personal and malicious is the infamous story of Archilochus' attack in verse on Lycambes, the father who first promised his daughter in marriage to the poet, then later recanted, and finally, because of the poet's ensuing iambics against him, was driven to commit suicide along with his two daughters.[24] This story has generally been perceived, by the ancients (including Martial) as well as moderns, as a personal attack by Archilochus on a real person for the purpose of revenge. Yet, while the story may (or may not) have a basis in a personal experience, it was versified by Archilochus primarily for the purpose of illustrating a general truth to his social community.[25] As Brown puts it:

> Lycambes is revealed as an oath-breaker and thus a menace to society; the daughters are exposed as sexually incontinent and so deserving of opprobrium. By subjecting his enemies to invective Archilochus seeks to protect the community. However personal the insult, Archilochus treats his feud with Lycambes as a matter of public concern, and this public aspect seems to lie very near the heart of ἴαμβος.[26]

In sum, it is easy to overlook the significance of these attacks on individuals: they are not primarily personal, but rather are illustrations given for the benefit of the social community by a person gifted in his understanding of human character and in his judicious and effective reporting of character flaws and social transgressions.[27] As Nagy expresses it (1989, 63):

> It is important to stress ... that the 'blaming' side of Archilochus was part of the poet's overall function as a socially redeeming exponent of song and poetry, one who blames what is ostensibly bad while he praises what is good. This socially redeeming value ... is a traditional civic function, viewed as integrating the community.

These attacks, then, were not so much personal and malicious as programmatic: wittily humorous assaults on a character-type in order to address and treat behaviour dangerous to the social community. Put another way, the specific purpose of the obscene and sexually graphic jokes in the iambic tradition, which was originally linked to ritual and religious festivities, was to recognize, celebrate, and reconnect the reader or listener with the basic human feelings, drives, and instincts and thus help the social community achieve and maintain a healthy and productive state.[28]

Roman invective

The distinguishing invective component of the Greek iambic tradition – the mocking and sometimes obscene jokes – surfaced in the Roman literary tradition in several forms:[29] besides in epigram (which includes Catullus, as discussed in the Introduction), it surfaced in personal and political polemic, attested from the time of Naevius; in humorous or satirical verse of popular origin, such as the scurrilous verses sung by soldiers at Roman triumphs; or *Fescennini*, songs of ribald abuse used at weddings and at harvest-festivals;[30] in Plautine comedy;[31] in mime; and finally, and especially, in satire. For example, Lucilius attacked enemies by name and reproached friends for social infractions (e.g. for not visiting the poet when he was sick).[32] Horace, likewise, although sidestepping the issue of attacking specific individuals, also used invective throughout in his *Satires* and *Epistles*, as did Persius and Juvenal in their poems.[33]

As for the purpose of these attacks, the Roman satirists uniformly contextualized and justified their invective in the same way: they argued that its real-life subject-matter and criticism were relevant and ethically beneficial to the reader, especially when compared to what poets in the so-called higher genres composed.[34] For example, Horace, via his poet-persona, dissociated himself from the company of poets (*Sat.* 1.4.38ff.):[35] instead he characterized himself as giving ethical instruction, as his father did for him, by pointing out examples of bad social behaviour in a playful way (*Sat.* 1.4.105-31).

Persius, of special note as Martial's near contemporary, illustrates even more strongly this ethical tone to his invective that marks it as beneficial, even necessary, for the health of the social community. For instance, in his first *Satire*, he, in setting out the principles, limits, and goals of the Roman satirist, attacks contemporary poets for their pretentiousness and love of notoriety. Then he attacks the horrible poetry being produced (e.g. 'all the dear little elegies improvised by crapulous grandees', 51-2);[36] also poetry that is devoid of truth because it may offend a patron; or poetry that is on effete, antiquated, or irrelevant themes; or, finally, poetry that is written in an affectedly fashionable style. After this vehement assault on the present state of literary affairs, the interlocutor, who fears the poet-persona will offend someone with his satire, asks him: 'but what's the need to irritate tender ears with biting truth?' The poet-persona at first acquiesces by agreeing to say that everything and everybody is fine (even though it is not so), but then, catching himself, replies in defence of his writing satire that Lucilius 'cut' the city and broke his molar in criticism of persons, and that sly Horace probed every fault and cleverly held up the public to his criticism. He, then, will also speak out, if only to his little book, and reveal his secret, a truth that he himself has seen. He will do this, as he says, because his secret is worth more than any *Iliad* (1.114-23).

Finally, there is Martial's nearest contemporary, Juvenal, who gave many of Martial's themes extended treatment.[37] Juvenal declares that he has taken up the writing of satire in opposition to the so-called higher genres, which treated subject-matter from Greek mythology instead of real-life characters and situations. His own brand of poetry, Juvenal claims, was forced from him in response to all the worthless verse he is forced to hear and especially in response to the outrageous vices and unjust practices of his society.[38] Thus does he, like the other Roman satirists (and Martial), present himself as outside the established literary tradition (e.g. epic and tragedy): rather he characterizes himself as a uniquely inspired and privileged poet who has chosen to write about real-life situations for the ethical benefit of his reader.[39] In short, Juvenal's style, which was both personal and forthright, his subject-matter, which was real-life characters and situations, and his avowed purpose or intent, which was to expose vice and injustice through attack, all recall the iambic tradition.

Martial's poetry has very much in common with satire, even beyond the invective component.[40] For instance, Martial, like the satirists Horace, Persius, and Juvenal, sets himself apart from the literary tradition of the so-called higher genres: for example, at epigram

8.3.13-18 he dismisses the works of writers of tragedy and epic – works that are fit only to become hated school texts, as he puts it – in order to continue writing epigram.[41] At epigram 4.49 Martial even more strongly distances himself from those who compose epics and tragedies: he claims that those writers who compose on the standard mythological themes that have nothing to do with reality are actually playing more at writing than he reputedly does with his light verse. Finally, at epigram 10.4, probably Martial's most mature statement of his literary programme, he again declares, in a contrast with the so-called higher genres whose subject-matter was Greek myth, that his poems deal with the real world.[42] He instructs his reader:

> hoc lege, quod possit dicere vita 'meum est'.
> non hic Centauros, non Gorgonas Harpyiasque
>   invenies: hominem pagina nostra sapit.
> Sed non vis, Mamurra, tuos cognoscere mores
>   nec te scire: legas Aetia Callimachi.

10.4.8-12

> Read this, of which life can say, 'It's mine'. Not here will you find Centaurs, Gorgons, and Harpies: our page smacks of humanity. But if you do not wish, Mamurra, to know human character or yourself, read the *Aetia* of Callimachus.

Martial here not only declares his poetry's general subject-matter – that he is writing about the daily activities and concerns of his audience – but also states the desired effect of his poetry:[43] readers can come to know human behaviour and also come to know themselves through the poet's treatment of real-world situations. Although the satirists imply that their poetry will benefit their readers in understanding proper behaviour, Martial's claim that he brings his readers to know others and themselves is unique in its specificity and directness. Thus does he justify his attacks on character types.

Martial's invective

Because Martial's epigrams contain so much invective, he is careful to explain and justify this controversial and potentially dangerous element.[44] Moreover, since his invective oftentimes utilizes obscenity and graphic sexual content (as is typical for invective in the iambic tradition), it requires further defence and justification.[45] Thus Martial begins his very first book with a long programmatic preface given entirely to the defence of both of these volatile elements of his poetry:

Spero me secutum in libellis meis tale temperamentum ut de illis queri non possit quisquis de se bene senserit, cum salva infimarum quoque personarum reverentia ludant; quae adeo antiquis auctoribus defuit ut nominibus non tantum veris abusi sint sed et magnis. Mihi fama vilius constet et probetur in me novissimum ingenium. Absit a iocorum nostrorum simplicitate malignus interpres ne epigrammata mea scribat: inprobe facit qui in alieno libro ingeniosus est. Lascivam verborum veritatem, id est epigrammaton linguam, excusarem, si meum esset exemplum: sic scribit Catullus, sic Marsus, sic Pedo, sic Gaetulicus, sic quicumque perlegitur. Si quis tamen tam ambitiose tristis est ut apud illum in nulla pagina latine loqui fas sit, potest epistola vel potius titulo contentus esse. Epigrammata illis scribuntur qui solent spectare Florales. Non intret Cato theatrum meum, aut si intraverit, spectet. Videor mihi meo iure facturus si epistolam versibus clusero:

Nosses iocosae dulce cum sacrum Florae
festosque lusus et licentiam volgi,
cur in theatrum, Cato severe, venisti?
an ideo tantum veneras, ut exires?

1 praefatio

I hope I have followed in my little books such a balance that no one who has a clear conscience can complain about them:[46] they have their fun, but with respect preserved for even the humblest persons. That respect was so lacking in ancient writers that they abused not only real people by name, but even great people. Let my fame come at a lesser cost, and may cleverness be the last thing that wins me approval. Let the malicious interpreter stay away from the straightforwardness of my jokes and not rewrite my epigrams. He acts improperly who is ingenious with another man's book. The playfully wanton realism of language, which is the language of epigram, I would justify if the precedent were mine: but thus writes Catullus, thus Marsus and Pedo and Gaetulicus, and whoever else is read right through. If, however, anyone is so ostentatiously sombre that Latin cannot be spoken on any page in his presence, he can be content with this letter, or rather with the title. Epigrams are written for those who are accustomed to watch Flora's festivities. Let Cato not enter my theatre, or if he does enter, let him watch. I imagine I shall act properly if I close my letter with some verse:

> Since you knew of the pleasant rite of jocose Flora,
> and the festive jokes and licence of the crowd,
> why did you come into the theatre, stern Cato?
> Or had you only come in so that you might walk out?

Part of Martial's concern in the opening of this preface is to avoid the resentment and anger of the emperor and other highly placed persons.[47] For very probably Martial is here reacting to the abusive invective of his self-acknowledged model, Catullus, who, writing in a different political environment – one that yet permitted personal attacks on political figures in poetry – used scurrilous verse on Caesar, Pompey, Mamurra, and Piso – all important, public figures who were alive when he wrote. Since Martial wrote under an emperor – and for most of his writing career under the especially careful (or insecure) Emperor Domitian, he is making clear that his invective – or his jokes, as he terms them – are not to be taken as attacks on community members, even if some choose to read them that way. As he puts it: 'Let the malicious interpreter stay away from the straightforwardness of my jokes and not rewrite my epigrams' (7-9).

Besides serving to protect him against a libel charge (or worse), Martial's declaration of his invective's *temperamentum* and his strong protests against misinterpretation and plagiarism also make clear to his readers that he knows the proper use for his invective: it is a tool to be used not indiscriminately or irresponsibly, but in the right spirit for the right purpose. Two other epigrams – although they have to do with verbal rather than written jokes – define fairly explicitly Martial's limits to his invective. At epigram 1.41 Martial targets one

Caecilius, who, although he believes himself to be *urbanus*, 'elegantly amusing', or 'witty', is rather, as Martial says, a *verna*, a '(spoiled) house-born slave' (1.41.2), who 'sports with insensible licence' (*ludit ... stolida procacitate*, 1.41.19).[48] Of course this runs counter to Martial's own claim to *temperamentum* – judicious use of invective – in his Book 1 preface.[49] Then, at epigram 6.44, Martial criticizes one Calliodorus, who believes that he jokes wittily, and also believes that he alone has abundant wit. Rather, Martial says in address to Calliodorus, 'you laugh at everyone, make jokes against all; thus you think you please as a dinner guest' (6.44.3-4). Calliodorus here plays the role of the *scurra*, the buffoon or parasite, who does not know tasteful restraint when joking that he will say anything about anybody in order to get a laugh and be invited back to dinner.[50] This indiscriminate joking also violates Martial's rule of *temperamentum*: he, unlike Callidorus, knows the limits to joking and will not violate them in order to get a meal.[51]

After using the first half of the preface to establish the legitimacy of his invective – that it will be used only in the proper way – Martial in the rest of the preface defends his use of 'playfully wanton realism of language' (*lasciva verborum veritas*, line 10) and his 'speaking in Latin' (*latine loqui*, line 15) – that is, his use of sexually graphic language and obscenity.[52] Martial's juxtaposition of invective and obscenity here reflects the close connection in his poems between the two: for example, the words he uses in his preface of his invective – the verb *ludere* (line 4) and its cognate noun, *lusus* (line 21), and the noun *iocus* (line 8) and adjective *iocosus* (line 20) – regularly imply a sexual context, usually with the use of obscenity.[53] In fact, much of Martial's invective does employ obscenity, and, conversely, most of the obscenity in Martial's poems comes in the context of his invective.[54]

Martial is unique in the large amount of obscenity and sexual content he has in his epigrams.[55] His defence of it in his preface to Book 1 (and elsewhere) reveals what it adds to his invective, as well as the target and purpose of that invective. He begins his defence by citing Catullus and other authors who set the precedent – a common and powerful argument for ancient Latin poets because of their reliance upon and respect for the literary tradition.[56] For example, Pliny the Younger, Martial's near contemporary, in defence of certain of his own epigrams that had indelicate subject-matter and 'plain language', notes that many distinguished and serious writers neither avoided

25

lascivious subjects nor refrained from expressing them *verbis nudis*, 'with unveiled words' (4.14.4). Then Pliny goes on to quote Catullus for the archetypal defence for such taboo matter:

> Nam castum esse decet pium poetam
> ipsum,versiculos nihil necesse est,
> qui tunc denique habent salem et leporem
> si sunt molliculi et parum pudici.
>
> Pliny 4.14.5 = Catull. 16.5-8

> It is proper for the sacred poet to be pure himself, but it is not necessary for his verse to be so. These verses only in the end have wit and charm if they are somewhat soft and have little of chastity.

Pliny, through this quotation, makes clear the main concern of writers who use obscenity in their verse: that they neither be judged too *mollis*, 'soft', or, in its metaphorical sense, 'effeminate' – that is, unmanly because of lack of control over their sexual appetites; nor considered immoral because their poetry's risqué language and content was thought to reflect their own character.[57]

Martial also addresses these concerns for his character elsewhere, but here in this preface he takes his defence of his obscene jokes a step further, thus showing his particular target and purpose for his obscene invective.[58] First, he describes the sort of person who would object to his poems' obscenity and sexual jokes: one who has carried the ideals of manliness and morality too far.[59] He specifically characterizes this person as so *ambitiose tristis*, so 'ostentatiously' or 'ambitiously stern' that he can not tolerate plain Latin (i.e. obscenity) on the page. *Tristis* is a key term that, along with the terms *gravis* and *severus*, Martial uses several times in various contexts to signify a temperament or attitude that he wishes to moderate or balance with his obscene jokes.[60] The adverb *ambitiose* indicates motive for the display of severity – namely, that the person makes him or herself conspicuous in order to gain favour or public acclaim. Then, to illustrate his objection, Martial marks out the proper boundaries or territory for his obscene poetry.[61] He does this by likening that type of poetry to the *Florales* (sc. *ludi*), the typically licentious games that

26

occurred during the annual spring festival in honour of the goddess Flora, an old, Italian vegetation goddess.[62] Flora, of course, can be compared to Demeter, the Greek agricultural goddess, whose rites also included obscene and abusive jokes, as initiated by Iambe in the *Hymn to Demeter* (see above). Already, then, in this opening preface Martial shows some similarity between his own poetry and that of the iambic tradition: specifically, just as Archilochus wrote abusive and obscene poetry that had been inspired by, and was descended from, the ritual jesting that was part of Demeter's rites, Martial wrote obscene jests that compare to the abusive and obscene verse used to honour Flora.[63]

Martial reinforces this link between his obscene jesting and that associated with the iambic tradition in other poems by comparing his jests to those used in other Roman festive events that are religious. For example, he compares his own abusive jests to the obscene and abusive songs that soldiers sang to a triumphing general (1.4.3-4; 7.8); to the marriage invocation, the *thalassio*, which contained obscenity and jests (1.35.6-7); and to the licence of the Roman festival of the Saturnalia (e.g. 4.14, 10.18, 11.2, and 11.15).[64] Martial's repeated references to specifically festive and religious occasions of which obscene jests were a part strongly suggest that, consciously or not, he was following in the iambic tradition.

After his comparison of his obscene jokes to those used in the Floralia, Martial in his preface to Book 1 continues with an illustration of someone who is too severe to allow for obscene jesting even in the proper context of religious festivities. He tells the story of Cato (Uticensis), who is one of the historical figures whom Martial and other Latin poets regularly used as representatives of the old Roman morality in its extreme degree.[65] The story is that back in 55 BCE during the Floralia Cato entered the theatre in which the mimes that contained obscene jokes and nudity were taking place.[66] Cato voluntarily left the theatre when, it is said, he perceived that his presence was inhibiting the actors from using obscenities and stripping off. His consideration of the audience's enjoyment gained Cato its support and respect, which it showed through applause for his action. Martial's remarks, however, and his pointed question in the last line of the poem indicate that Cato knew exactly what he would encounter before he entered the theatre, and thus entered only to make a show of his morality.[67] Of course, the further implication of the story is that any reader who would now object to Martial's poems' obscene jokes and sexual content is, like Cato, being self-righteous and overly severe since Martial is giving warning here at the outset of their content. Martial's target, then, as demonstrated here, is a moral or ethical earnestness or even zealousness that was, in Martial's mind, potentially hypocritical.

Martial's regular association of his verse, and particularly his obscene jokes, with another Roman festival, the Saturnalia, shows again as his target a morality that was over-zealous and too severe; it also reveals more of the purpose of his obscene jokes.[68] A good example of his association of his verse with the Saturnalia comes near the beginning of Book 11, a book which was written specifically for that festival as well as to mark the accession of the new emperor, Nerva.[69] In this particular poem Martial gives his reader notice – either as a warning or an enticement – that Book 11 has more than the usual amount of obscenity and sexual content:

Sunt chartae mihi quas Catonis uxor
et quas horribiles legant Sabinae:
his totus volo rideat libellus
et sit nequior omnibus libellis,
qui vino madeat nec erubescat
pingui sordidus esse Cosmiano,
ludat cum pueris, amet puellas,
nec per circuitus loquatur illam,
ex qua nascimur, omnium parentem,
quam sanctus Numa mentulam vocabat.
versus hos tamen esse tu memento
Saturnalicios, Apollinaris:
mores non habet hic meos libellus.

11.15

I have little books that Cato's wife and fearsome Sabine women could read; but I want this whole book to laugh and be naughtier than all my little books. Let it be soaked with wine and not blush to be greasy with rich Cosmian pomade; let it sport with the boys; let it love the girls; let it name outright that from which we are born, the parent of all, that which holy Numa used to call cock.

28

But remember that these verses are Saturnalian, Apollonaris: this little book does not have my morals.

Here again Martial contrasts the licence of his poetry – with its sexual content and obscenity – to a strict morality, as represented by Cato's wife and by the 'fearsome Sabine women', who were often used exemplars of a strict morality in literature.[70] In defence of his licence Martial enlists the revered Numa, an early Roman king, who, although noted for his religiosity and strong character, still was able to use a primary obscenity.[71] The implication is that a degree of licence is permissible and even desirable, since Numa himself evidenced it. Martial further counters this overly strict morality by comparing its licence to treat sexual matters and use forthright language with that of the Roman festival of the Saturnalia.[72] For the Saturnalia was especially characterized by its general licence:[73] for example, the toga was exchanged for informal dinner dress, and both gambling and drinking were permitted; also there was much banqueting, which included light verse as entertainment, replete with obscene jokes.[74] Indeed, Martial's verse suited the tone of the Saturnalia so well that some if not a good deal of his own verse was written specifically for recitation during the festival – that is, as entertainment for dinner parties occurring during the holiday.[75]

The nature of the festival of the Saturnalia provides an explanation for the licence of speech and sexual content characteristic of it. The key is that the Saturnalia, like its namesake, Saturn, is very probably agricultural in function.[76] As such, the obscene jokes associated with it would be, as in the rites and festivities of Demeter and Flora, intended as apotropaic (meant to ward off evil) and also as sympathetic magic – that is, meant to induce fertility in the crops, as exemplified in the *Hymn to Demeter* (see above).[77] Likewise with the other festivities to which Martial refers in his defence of obscene jests – triumphs and marriage invocations: the purpose of the obscene jests is apotropaic or to induce fertility.

What do these two purposes of the obscene jokes of the Saturnalian festival (and the other festivals as well) imply about the effect of Martial's obscene jokes? The fertility in crops normally induced by the obscene jokes typical of an agricultural festival could in Martial's literary and social context signify a fecundity of a general sort – that is, a promotion of creativity in a sphere not agricultural. For example, Martial's obscene jokes could be in corrective balance to the stagnation and the eventual degradation and even perversion that too severe and restricted a social and moral ethic bring, as exemplified by Cato and excessively strict types. In other words, Martial's obscene jokes could function to reconnect the reader to an earthy vitality that renewed and inspired, just as Iambe used obscene jokes to break through to Demeter.[78] Without that renewal – that reconnecting with the basic human feelings, drives, and instincts – the social community would stagnate in its moral severity.

Finally, epigram 1.35, a defence of Martial's poems' obscene jokes and sexual content, sums up well Martial's target and the effect of these obscenities:

> Versus scribere me parum severos
> nec quos praelegat in schola magister,
> Corneli, quereris: sed hi libelli,
> tamquam coniugibus suis mariti,
> non possunt sine mentula placere.
> quid si me iubeas thalassionem
> verbis dicere non thalassionis?
> quis Floralia vestit et stolatum
> permittit meretricibus pudorem?
> lex haec carminibus data est iocosis,
> ne possint, nisi pruriant, iuvare.
> quare deposita severitate
> parcas lusibus et iocis rogamus,
> nec castrare velis meos libellos.
> Gallo turpius est nihil Priapo.

1.35

Cornelius, you complain that I write verses not austere enough and not the sort a schoolmaster would dictate in class. But these little books are like husbands with their wives – they can't please without a cock. You might as well tell me to sing a wedding song without using wedding song words. Does anybody clothe Flora's festivities and allow prostitutes the modesty of the matron's robe? There's a law laid down for joking verse: it can't be good for anything unless it sexually itches. So please put strictness aside and spare my playfulness and jokes. Don't try to castrate my little books. There's nothing uglier than a neutered Priapus.

Martial's verses are accused of being *parum severi*. *Severus* is yet another term that, along with the terms *gravis* and *tristis*, Martial uses to target that too severe ethic which he redresses with his obscene jokes.[79] As usual Martial makes his attack through a series of telling images. First, he compares his poems' sexual content to husbands' *mentulae*, without which wives would not be able to be pleased.[80] The comparison suggests fertility, both through Martial's titillation of the reader with the idea of a wife taking pleasure in her husband's penis, and also with the image of the *mentula*, which signifies, as it often did for the ancient Greeks and Romans, fertility.[81] Similarly, the next image Martial uses for his obscenity – the *thalassio*, the ancient marriage invocation whose obscenity and sexual content were meant to induce the conception of children – again bears out the connection between his obscene jokes and fertility.[82]

The third image that Martial uses – that of 'clothing the Floralia' – recalls his defence in his preface to Book 1, where he compared his epigrams to the festivities of the Floralia – specifically, the mime shows that contained obscene jest and sexual content. Here at epigram 1.35 he adds to the image by pointing up just how ridiculous it would be to remove the elements of sexuality and obscenity from an agricultural festival intended to induce fertility. Thus again Martial makes the connection between obscene jokes and fertility.

Finally, at the end of epigram 1.35, Martial uses the figure of Priapus to epitomize his poems' obscene jests and sexual content. Priapus was an ithyphallic divinity of Greek origin, said to be the son of Dionysus – the god to which he is most closely linked – by either a nymph or Aphrodite herself.[83] His cult was centred in the Lampsacus region, from which it spread, from the third century BCE on, and he had associations with primitive apotropaic and fertility rituals. He was associated with sexuality, human fertility, and gardens and their protection: specifically, he would use his phallus in order to ward off and punish intruders. In ancient Roman literature Priapus was taken up by the neoterics, including Catullus, Martial's avowed model, and then by the satirists and the authors of *Priapea*.[84] These literary

31

sources portrayed him most often as a rustic, agricultural deity, a guardian of crops, groves, and vineyards, and thus he can be compared to Demeter because of his associations with fertility.[85] Most often in post-Augustan literature he played the role of *custos hortorum*, 'guardian of the gardens', a minatory figure whose purpose was both to defend against and to punish transgressors.[86] Thus, in this poem Martial seems to be asking here how Priapus could do his job of protecting the garden: for to turn him into a Gallus – a priest of Cybele who had both his testicles and penis removed – would be to render him weaponless.[87]

Yet, Priapus' treatment elsewhere in ancient Roman poetry (including in Martial) suggests a more fundamental sense to this Priapic image – something that runs more in accord with the other images in this particular poem and his similarity to Demeter.[88] For in the literature he is rarely portrayed as the *successful* protector and punisher; much more often he is presented, for the purpose of amusement, as the over-sexed and more than amply endowed would-be punisher/seducer of those in his garden.[89] Thus, although part of Priapus' role was to guard the garden and punish transgressors, his primary function, as symbolized by his over-sized phallus and libido, was to make that garden fertile and keep it productive. In other words, Priapus primarily represents or embodies the drive to procreate rather than the drive to protect, since he is rarely portrayed as successful at the latter, and consistently represented as preoccupied with the former. Thus this fourth image of Priapus, like the other three images, highlights the connection between Martial's obscene jokes and fertility.

Some general conclusions, now, about the nature and effect of Martial's invective. First, he disavows the malicious and personal attack. Rather, he targets, as he tells us, various vices – never any particular practitioner, and always with the purpose of delighting and entertaining according to what is socially acceptable. Hence, he presents and uses his invective in just the way the Roman satirists did: he claims the right or privilege to target examples of degenerative behaviour because he does it with no malicious intent, but rather to entertainingly instruct and benefit his social community. Such a socially oriented rationale and effect show his poetry's connection with the iambic tradition. Also, Martial's poetry's obscene and sexually graphic invective has a specific target: with it he attacks Roman *gravitas* or *severitas* carried to a stifling and hypocritical degree, which makes it dangerous to the social community. In this he followed his avowed model, Catullus, in that both poets used the tools of primary obscenity and graphic sexual content in their invective to break through the formality and seriousness that so characterized Roman culture.[90] This strong emphasis on the visceral and primal underside of human nature – normally kept rigorously controlled and hidden – is the counteraction to this Roman penchant for the serious. The effect, then, of Martial's obscene jokes was to open up the psyche for refreshment, renewal, and rebirth, just as Iambe did for Demeter, and thereby maintain the community's health and productivity. Thus, with his invective, and in particular with its uniquely large amount of obscenity and sexual content, he affirms his connection with the iambic tradition.

2

Amicitia

> We need a discussion and classification of beneficial acts, the
> thing which most ties together human society.
>
> Seneca, de Ben. 1.4.2

The workings of interpersonal relationships, generically termed by the
ancient Romans as *amicitia*, 'friendship', in its wide range of senses –
from the emperor-subject relationship, to the patron-client relationship, to the casual or professional relationship, to the relationship
between dearest friends – is one of Martial's most prominent and
pervasive themes. No surprise, since he is writing *vers de société*, verse
that was a commentary on the social views and practices of his
readership, that he would be much concerned with *amicitia*, the basis
upon which the ancient Roman social community was built and maintained.[1] Martial's representation of *amicitia*, however, is bound to
confuse and even alienate many readers today. For he most often
focuses on the protocol of reciprocity between individuals – the exchange of goods and services that was so characteristic of ancient
Greek and Roman interpersonal relations, and was its most visible
proof. Unfortunately, many readers mistake Martial's emphasis on
the exchange inherent in *amicitia* for something else: they usually
take it for nothing less than a form of extortion, with the poet-persona
most often playing the role of a mercenary client who is milking his
patron.[2] The actual effect of Martial's representation of friendship was
to encourage at a communal and not personal level the trust between
individuals that was necessary for social exchange and a strong social
community.

Reciprocity and friendship

David Konstan, in his introduction to his book on friendship in the
classical world, perceptively informs his reader that the concept of

friendship has changed so much over the years that it is an historical variable – in other words, every age defines (and limits) friendship in its own way.[3] He then devotes some pages to explaining the most recent European-American conception of friendship, which has especially been influenced by the anthropological emphasis on systems of exchange in pre-modern societies.[4] This anthropological approach to friendship, as articulated by the classicist Moses Finley and then his disciples, was predicated upon the premise that

> the societies of classical Greece and Rome did not possess an economy in the modern sense of the term. Rather, the economy was inextricably embedded in a complex of social relations that included personal bonds.
>
> Konstan 1997, 4

In other words, because the economies of classical Greece and Rome did not have the integrative and distributive capability of market and state – such as exist today, for example, in Europe and America – vital resources had to be obtained largely through personal relations.[5] More specifically as applied to friendship, this view maintains that the ancient Greeks and Romans formed and maintained interpersonal relationships so that they could exchange goods and services not available to them in any other way.[6] Today, then, most scholars, basing their views in this anthropological methodology, believe that ancient Greek and Roman friendship was predicated on reciprocity more than on mutual affection, and that the quality of intimacy, which is normally part of modern friendship, was not necessary for friendship in the ancient Greek and Roman world.[7]

How accurate is this anthropologically based perception of ancient friendship as predicated on reciprocity? Certainly the ancient Greeks and Romans recognized reciprocity as an integral part of friendship.[8] For example, Aristotle says in his explication of the types of friendship, that in all types there is a reciprocity or exchange inherent in the relationship: even in the case of the so-called highest type of friendship – that which is based on respect for virtue or character – those involved 'must love in equal measure and create a balance in other ways [i.e. "by being good or pleasant or useful"]'.[9]

This concept of reciprocity through exchange is omnipresent in all types of ancient Greek and Roman interpersonal relationships. For instance, it goes all the way back to Homeric literature: in Book 6 of the *Iliad* (119ff.), for example, Glaucus and Diomedes, when they discover that their grandfathers had established the bond of ξενία with an exchange of gifts, decline to fight and instead exchange armour right there while the battle rages around them. Another good example comes in the final book of the *Odyssey*. Odysseus in the recognition scene with his father says to Laertes (before Laertes has come to know that he is speaking with his son Odysseus) that years ago he took Laertes' son into his house and gave him gifts of friendship. Laertes replies that the countless gifts given to his son were bestowed in vain, for, 'If you had found him alive in the land of Ithaca, he would have sent you on your way with gifts in return, and given good hospitality, as is proper for whoever has given' (24.284-5).

Ancient Roman literature likewise substantiates the importance of reciprocity to interpersonal relationships. Indeed, the frequency and length of treatment of the topic by Roman authors gives an indication of just how unique and pivotal reciprocity was to the workings of friendship in Roman society – seemingly more so than with ancient Greek society.[10] For instance, Cicero in his essay on friendship states that, although he sees friendship as springing from the natural inclination of the soul to love and be affectionate rather than from calculation of what the friendship will bring, mutual interchange is really characteristic of friendship (*de Amic.* 26-7). Seneca goes even further in his seven-book-long treatise on the nature and rules of the exchange of *beneficia*, by which he meant favours or gifts in the form of goods and services that were characteristic of friendship.[11] He calls the practice of bestowing *beneficia* 'that which most binds together human society' and condemns ingratitude as actually worse than murder and the source of the worst crimes.[12] Thus, for Seneca, the protocol of reciprocity was a topic worthy of much discussion. As he puts it:

> We need a discussion and classification of beneficial acts, the thing which most ties together human society. A law must be established so that thoughtless indulgence that has the appearance of generosity not be acceptable. A law must be established, too, so that this regulation itself not restrain liberality, which

neither ought to be lacking nor overabundant, while it tempers it. We need to be taught to give freely, to accept freely, to make return freely; and to establish a high standard, whereby we not only equal in deed and spirit the ones to whom we are obligated, but surpass them. For he who is under obligation to return a favour never catches up to it unless he surpasses it.

de Ben. 1.4.2-4

Seneca's strong emphasis on the protocol of reciprocity indicates how much a part it was of interpersonal relationships or *amicitia* – how it took on a life of its own, so to speak, so that its workings and ethics in large part defined interpersonal relationships for the Romans. Indeed, Seneca was not treating the subject of friendship in his long treatise; rather he was analysing the exchange of goods and services inherent in interpersonal relationships and how that process of exchange tied society together.[13] When Seneca does speak about what were clearly altruistic friendships (see below), reciprocity, though it always figures as part of the relationship, was definitely not the reason for, or purpose of, the friendship. Indeed, a closer look at the ancient sources shows that reciprocity, although for the ancient Greeks and Romans an integral part of altruistic friendship, was clearly not the ideological reason for it.

Aristotle, for example, defines three types of friendship.[14] All three types have their basis in the reciprocal and mutually known goodwill (εὔνοι) of the participants for one another, with the basis or cause of that goodwill stemming from three sources – hence, the three types of friendship: virtue, pleasure, and utility. Thus friends whose goodwill or affection is based on utility – the so-called lowest type of friendship – love each other only for the benefits that come from each other, and not for what they are in and of themselves. Similarly, for friendships based on pleasure, the parties love each other only because of the pleasure derived from the other party. Friendships of these two types tend not to be permanent or long-lasting, since the parties change and are no longer useful to one another, or the tastes of the parties change, and they are no longer pleasurable to one another. In the so-called perfect type of friendship, however, the relationship is based on the virtue of the two parties, and the parties wish good to each other for each other's sake rather than their own sake. Thus, this highest type of friendship is altruistic in nature, and the reciprocity inherent in it is not the reason for its existence.

Similarly, Cicero distinguishes altruistic friendship (*amicitia*) from utilitarian relationships. He says that true friendship

> springs from nature rather than from need, from an inclination of the soul with a certain feeling of love rather than from calculation of how much usefulness the friendship is likely to have.[15]

In another passage he puts it even more bluntly:

> If people think that friendship arises from weakness and in order to secure someone through whom we might get what we desire, they leave her ... a humble and very low pedigree indeed, and take her as the daughter of poverty and indigence.[16]

Thus, simple reciprocity – the exchange of goods and services within an interpersonal relationship, although certainly characteristic of friendship, did not make friendship in its highest form.[17] Indeed, friendship in its truest or highest form was considered by Aristotle and Cicero as a rare thing – achievable with only one or two people in a lifetime.[18]

Finally, Seneca also defines true friendship as based on something other than reciprocity – namely, each party tries to benefit the other. As he puts it in high dramatic style:

> For what purpose do I get a friend? So that I have someone for whom I may die, so that I have someone whom I may follow into exile, against whose death I may set and lay out my own.
>
> *Ep.* 9.10

Seneca opposes this concept of friendship to that of entering a relationship in order to benefit oneself. He sees friendships such as these, which he says are commonly called temporary (*temporariae*), are short-term because once the original usefulness of the relationship is gone, the friendship itself ends (*Ep.* 9.8-9).

In contrast to these ancient ideals of altruistic friendship, however, stand the myriad examples in the ancient literature of what appear to be utilitarian friendships, usually termed today as patron-client relationships, and in which the exchange of goods and services, and not mutual affection, was central. For instance, Aristotle's two lower types of friendship – those based on utility and pleasure – have reciprocity as their primary basis: the parties form and maintain the relationship only for the exchange of pleasure, or goods and services; and if the exchange for some reason ceases, the relationship ends (*Eth. Nic.* 1156a14-24/8.3.2-4). Likewise, in the ancient Roman tradition, there was a range in types of *amicitia*: some altruistic in nature, but the majority having their basis in reciprocity.[19] Because of this range in types of interpersonal relations, confusion arises especially over the many poems in Martial's collection in which reciprocity is stressed in speaking of friendship.

Martial's *amicitia*: what is it?

Martial's representation of *amicitia* strongly brings out its inherently contradictory nature: that although it was ideally based on mutual and selfless affection, it evidenced and proved itself through an equitable exchange of goods and services.[20] For example, at epigram 2.55 Martial succinctly states the two possible and seemingly antithetical bases of an interpersonal relationship – bases that set up the inherent paradox of *amicitia*:

> Vis te, Sexte, coli: volebam amare.
> parendum est tibi: quod iubes, coleris.
> sed si te colo, Sexte, non amabo.

2.55

> You wish, Sextus, that I cultivate you. I was wanting to love you. It must be done as you bid: you will be cultivated. Yet if I cultivate you, Sextus, I'll not love you.

With the contrast between the two verbs, *colere*, 'to cultivate' or 'court' (i.e. 'cater to'), and *amare*, 'to love' or 'esteem', Martial distinctly differentiates between two exclusive types of interpersonal relations. The one type, designated by *colere*, is based primarily on reciprocity and personal gain in that Sextus seems only to be looking for attention and service from the poet, and not companionship – that is, he wants a strictly utilitarian relationship.[21] The other type, designated by *amare*, is a relationship based on selfless mutual respect, affection, and esteem – that is, the poet seems to want an altruistic friendship.

In several other poems Martial also makes a clear distinction between altruistic and strictly utilitarian relationships. For example, at epigram 4.40 he says in address to Postumus (assumed fictitious):

> Atria Pisonum stabant cum stemmate toto
>   et docti Senecae ter numeranda domus,
> praetulimus tantis solum te, Postume, regnis:
>   pauper eras et eques, sed mihi consul eras.
> tecum ter denas numeravi, Postume, brumas:
>   communis nobis lectus et unus erat.
> iam donare potes, iam perdere, plenus honorum,
>   largus opum: expecto, Postume, quid facias.
> nil facis, et serum est alium mihi quaerere regem.
>   hoc, Fortuna, placet? 'Postumus imposuit'.
>
> 4.40

When the halls of the Pisos were standing with all their pedigree and the thrice distinguished house of learned Seneca, I put you alone, Postumus, before such great patronage. You were poor and a knight, but to me you were a consul. With you, Postumus, I counted out thirty winter solstices. We shared one dining-couch. Now you are able to give, to squander – you, full of honours, abundant in resources. I await what you will do, Postumus. You do nothing, and it is too late for me to find another patron. Does this please you, Fortune? 'Postumus has cheated (me)!'

Here Martial compares the addressee, Postumus, to the families of the Pisos and Seneca, both wealthy, acknowledged patrons of the arts and whom Martial here terms as *regnis* (3), literally, 'royalty', but used here with the sense of 'patronage'.[22] Similarly, at line 9 he uses the term *rex*, 'king', but here with the sense of 'patron', thus making it clear that he is speaking of a utilitarian or patron-client relationship with Postumus. Finally, the accusation of Postumus having cheated – *imposuit* (10) – indicates that the relationship was based primarily on reciprocity rather than altruism. Thus, Martial again, as in epigram 2.55, plays upon the paradoxical nature of friendship: he contrasts the altruistic nature of his own feelings for Postumus – shown by the relationship's long length (thirty years) and its intimacy (dined together on the same couch – i.e. as equals) and its non-utilitarian nature (Martial attended Postumus when Postumus was unable to reciprocate as a true patron would), with Postumus' seemingly calculated and ungrateful behaviour, as he wittily characterizes with the closing words of the poem, 'Postumus has cheated (me)!'

Martial and other Roman poets, however, rarely drew such clear lines in their poems between altruistic and utilitarian friendships. Indeed, the very terminology Martial and others usually used for interpersonal relationships blurred the line between the types of relationships. For like other early imperial Roman writers, Martial avoided the status-laden terms *patronus*, *rex*, *dominus*, and *cliens* to designate the parties of a strictly utilitarian relationship because of the social stigma attached to those terms.[23] Much more frequently Martial used the inoffensive language of *amicitia* to designate the parties of all types of interpersonal relationships.[24] Yet, despite Martial's use of the language of *amicitia*, some of these poems certainly describe a utilitarian relationship: namely, a person of unequal social standing seeking to attach himself to a wealthy person primarily for the purpose of some sort of support or gain. To complicate matters further, although there is a ranking of grades of friendship in Roman literature, by and large the nature of the mutual commitments of each party was formally undefined and open-ended, and the two parties were usually not distinguished in social rank at all.[25] One final complication: there was an overlap between the services provided by *clientes* and *amici*. For example, both friends of equal or nearly equal standing as well as *clientes* might perform the *salutatio* – the early morning attendance of one person at the house of the other.[26] For all these reasons the line between altruistic and utilitarian friendship in Martial's poems is not at all distinct.

Epigram 10.58 is an excellent illustration of the confusion that can thus arise over Martial's representation of *amicitia* because of the blurring of the line between an altruistic and a utilitarian relationship. In this poem he addresses Sextus Julius Frontinus, a wealthy and accomplished statesman of consular rank, as well as a writer:[27]

2. Amicitia

Anxuris aequorei placidos, Frontine, recessus
　　et propius Baias litoreamque domum,
et quod inhumanae cancro fervente cicadae
　　non novere nemus, flumineosque lacus
dum colui, doctas tecum celebrare vacabat
　　Pieridas; nunc nos maxima Roma terit.
hic mihi quando dies meus est? iactamur in alto
　　urbis, et in sterili vita labore perit,
dura suburbani dum iugera pascimus agri
　　vicinosque tibi, sancte Quirine, lares.
sed non solus amat qui nocte dieque frequentat
　　limina nec vatem talia damna decent.
per veneranda mihi Musarum sacra, per omnes
　　iuro deos: et non officiosus amo.

10.58

When I dwelt in the calm retreat of Anxur by the sea, Frontinus,
and in a town house on the beach – a Baian villa closer to Rome,
and in a wood that the cruel cicadas, when Cancer blazes, did not
know, and a river-like canal, there was time to cultivate with you
the learned Pierides. Now greatest Rome wears us out. Here how
much of the day is my own? I am tossed in the city's ocean and
life wears itself out with sterile labour, while we feed oppressive
acres of suburban land and a dwelling neighbouring yours, holy
Quirinus. But he is not the only one who loves who frequents
doorsteps day and night; nor is such loss of time suitable for a
poet. By the venerable rites of the Muses, by all the gods I swear:
although not dutiful, I love you.

Frontinus is a wealthy and highly distinguished statesman. The poet,
as the reader infers from the last line, is expected to perform *officia*,
'services' or 'duties', such as attending Frontinus at the morning
salutation, accompanying him during the day, or coming to dinner.
Were they actual friends, or were they patron and client?

　　Probably most readers today would see this relationship between
the poet and Frontinus as a utilitarian-based or patron-client relationship.[28] Indeed, one is practically forced into that view by present day
notions of patronage. A good part of the problem, however, as Peter

43

White has argued, is that the term patronage has had a post-classical development of sense and connotation.[29] Specifically, White says of the terms clientage and patronage: (1) they imply a social gulf between the parties of the relationship that did not really exist; (2) they 'tend to suggest a formal arrangement based on reciprocal rights and obligations, rather than on the more elusive promptings of liberality and personal esteem'; and (3), they 'may create the impression that non-material forms of assistance, like protection before the law, were more important to the friends of the rich than pecuniary benefits' (1982, 57-8). None of these presuppositions, as White maintains, fits the situation of so-called client characters found in first-century CE literature.[30]

Moreover, in several other epigrams Martial contrasts the altruistic ideal of giving or sharing one's possessions with one's friends, with giving only for the sake of getting, thus indicating that interpersonal relationships were for him not so much a formal arrangement based on reciprocal rights and obligations (i.e. patronage), but rather were predicated upon esteem or affection. Outstanding examples are the several 'gifts as hooks' poems, which, like epigrams 2.55 and 4.40, are in general ethical expositions on friendship.[31] For example, at epigram 5.18, Martial denies that he is stingy or ungracious because he sends only poems as gifts at the Saturnalia instead of the more usual fare of linen, spoons, wax tapers, etc. His reason for sending only poems is, as he states:

> odi dolosas munerum et malas artes:
> imitantur hamos dona: namque quis nescit
> avidum vorata decipi scarum musca?
> quotiens amico diviti nihil donat,
> o Quintiane, liberalis est pauper.
>
> 5.18.6-10

I hate the deceitful and evil trickery of presents. Gifts are like hooks: for who doesn't know that the greedy sea-fish is taken in by the fly he has devoured? Whenever he gives nothing to a wealthy friend, Quintianus, a poor man is generous.

The ethical transgression pointed up here, as in all the 'gifts as hooks' poems, is that the gift-giver cares more about personal, material gain than about the friendship itself.[32] Martial, by showing himself aware of the mercenary business of using wealthy friends, instructs his reader in the ethics of friendship.

Epigram 7.86 is another even more dramatic condemnation of the abuse of the ethics of friendship and reciprocity:

> Ad natalicias dapes vocabar,
> essem cum tibi, Sexte, non amicus.
> quid factum est, rogo, quid repente factum est,
> post tot pignora nostra, post tot annos
> quod sum praeteritus vetus sodalis?
> sed causam scio. nulla venit a me
> Hispani tibi libra pustulati
> nec levis toga nec rudes lacernae.
> non est sportula quae negotiatur;
> pascis munera, Sexte, non amicos.
> iam dices mihi 'vapulet vocator'.

7.86

I was invited to your birthday banquet when I was not your friend, Sextus. What has happened, I ask, what has suddenly happened after so many of our pledges, after so many years, that I, an old companion, am passed over? Yet I know the reason. No pound of refined Spanish silver came to you from me nor a smooth toga nor an unused cloak. Hospitality is not something that is negotiated. You feed presents, Sextus, not friends. Now you will tell me, 'My secretary will be whipped'.

In this variation of 'gifts as hooks' poems, Sextus' birthday feast guest list is dictated by material gain and not friendship; or, as Martial puts it, Sextus' hospitality is negotiated – truly a relationship based on reciprocity. Note again Martial's use of *vetus sodalis*, 'old companion', for the poet-persona – his strongest phrasing for a friend, which, like epigrams 2.55 and 4.40, helps point up the paradoxical nature of friendship.[33]

Yet, in spite of all these poems that show Martial's awareness of the distinction between cultivating a person and loving a person, and in spite of his condemnation of the using of friends for personal gain in his ethical expositions, the long-standing textbook perception of Martial's poet-persona as a beggar-client still stands. Indeed, readers see his ethical expositions on friendship as just another layer of deception in his attempt to extort more from his patrons. Preconceived notions of friendship and patronage run too deep, and also the critical reader, understandably so, is reluctant to take the poet-persona's word for anything. Thus, something more is needed to understand the social context for Martial's poems on *amicitia*.

Social exchange

The modern day theory of social exchange can help the reader to get a better understanding of Martial's representation of *amicitia*: this theory goes beyond any cultural and historical preconceptions of friendship by focusing on the basic and universal processes and motives of social associations.[34] Moreover, it closely mirrors ancient Greco-Roman views of interpersonal relations. For example, Peter Blau, one of exchange theory's pioneers, traces the theory's roots to the ancient concept of friendship, as defined by Aristotle.[35] Blau quotes from the *Nicomachean Ethics*, which he maintains deals extensively with social exchange, from a passage where Aristotle is defining types of utilitarian friendships; specifically, Aristotle is here distinguishing between a moral (i.e. non-contractual) and legal (contractual and/or economic) relationship:

> [The moral type] is not based on stated terms, but the gift or other service is given as to a friend, although the giver expects to receive an equivalent or greater return, as though it had not been a free gift but a loan.[36]

Because of social exchange theory's roots in ancient thought and because it uses such an objective approach, it seems the right tool for analysing Martial's representation of *amicitia*.

As for the theory itself, the basic assumption behind social exchange is that people enter into social associations in order to satisfy wants that can only be supplied through social interaction (e.g., contentment in love, intellectual stimulation, professional recognition, the need for acceptance, the lust for power).[37] Rewards of these social associations may be intrinsic, humanitarian and spiritual, as in love or sociability; or extrinsic, such as goods and services sought for personal advantage and emotional satisfaction. Most social associations bring rewards that fall intermediate between these two extremes, but social exchange always includes intrinsic rewards. For its intrinsic element – the sentiments of affection, approval, and respect – distinguish it from a strictly economic transaction. Yet, its focus on benefits of extrinsic value – through the implicit or explicit bargaining for personal advantage – distinguishes it from the mutual attraction and support in profound love. In general, Blau characterizes social exchange as the basis for the large majority of interpersonal relationships, since the extremes, relationships based on pure calculation of advantage and those that are a pure expression of love, are rare (1964, 112).

The actual process of social exchange theory is as follows: one party obligates another with a gift, which can be goods or services. Since there is no contract involved, the original gift-giver attempts with the gift to create a bond based on trust, the creation of which is a major function of social exchange. The party who receives the gift must reciprocate in kind or lose status: if you cannot or do not respond to the social obligation created by the gift, you lose prestige.[38] This whole process of social exchange follows a protocol, as established by the particular culture, although this protocol is entirely informal or unwritten (unlike an economic exchange with its formal contract). Thus if a party breaks the rules – for example, does not reciprocate in kind, or responds too hastily or not at all – that party risks being ostracized socially, but of course no legal action could be taken.[39]

There is a tendency to be suspicious of interpersonal relationships based on exchange or reciprocity because of the fear that such relationships are strictly self-serving or mercenary at the worst. Yet the idea of reciprocity in social and interpersonal relationships is fundamental to civilized life: the ethical and moral codes of various cultures consistently contain the idea of reciprocity (e.g. 'Do unto others as you would have them do unto you'). Exchange theory embodies that basic pattern of behaviour: it premises that the parties involved in a relationship first establish the relationship through the exchange goods and services and then weigh (consciously or unconsciously) the relationship according to the equity of that and subsequent exchanges. This does

47

not mean that persons typically enter into a social exchange in order to maximize their own profits or gains; nor does it preclude altruistic friendships.[40] Rather, it says that an equitable exchange between the parties is a necessary part of establishing and maintaining an interpersonal relationship; indeed, an inequitable exchange – that is, one not satisfying to both parties – would result in the termination of a relationship.

Social exchange theory's strong emphasis on the reciprocity inherent in interpersonal relationships echoes the same strong emphasis on reciprocity found in the ancient sources. Yet, surprisingly enough, the actual major function of social exchange is not the acquisition of goods and services. Indeed, in a social exchange parties cannot even count on receiving benefits in return, nor can they stipulate what types of benefits they desire in return or when they require them; furthermore, some of the most important benefits of social exchange, such as social approval and respect, do not have a material value that can be priced exactly.[41] Since, then, the recipient of the initial gift or service decides when and how to reciprocate, if at all, social exchange requires trust of the participants. Moreover, a social exchange generally evolves slowly so that trust can be built incrementally without too great a risk: thus the exchange of goods and services generally proceeds at a slow rate.

Given the non-contractual nature of social exchange that makes counting on certain returns impossible, and given the slowly evolving and risk-laden process required to establish it, what then is social exchange's major function, if it is not the acquisition of goods and services? As Blau puts it, since any return in a social exchange comes at the discretion of the participants (and not according to any bargaining or formal contract), social exchange's fundamental significance is for developing bonds of trust and friendship (1974, 210). To put it differently, the exchange of goods and services, even if begun solely out of self-interest and on a small scale, generates trust in social relations through the recurrence and escalation (in value) of the exchange (Blau 1964, 94). Indeed, sometimes the benefits exchanged are valued more as symbols of the underlying mutual trust and support they express, which is the main concern of the participants (Blau 1964, 95).

Building mutual trust, then, underlies social exchange and is its primary objective. This mutual trust in turn creates social currency or social capital, as it has been popularly termed: a network of acquaintances and friends that can be relied upon for benefits that range from emotional support, like companionship, to gifts of cash.[42] In other words, the participants in a social exchange are more concerned with building and maintaining community than they are with the goods and services exchanged. As Gold, in speaking of gift giving and reciprocity present in 'Flavian patronage' says: 'The gift in this kind of exchange is less important as an object than for its symbolic value and its ability to create and maintain community.'[43]

Fides

According to this model of social exchange, then, Martial's underlying and guiding focal point in his representations of friendship would be the establishing of trust, *fides*, between the parties and not the acquisition of goods and services.[44] Seneca testifies to the great importance of *fides*: he says we possess our wealth only temporarily – that we are only procurators of our possessions, and that the only way we can be sure of our wealth is by giving gifts (*dona danda*).[45] Cicero likewise attests directly to the centrality of *fides* not only in friendship but in human affairs in general:

> [I]n matters to which we ourselves cannot attend, trust [*fides*] delegated to friends is substituted for our own labours; whoever violates this trust attacks the common safeguard of all and, as far as he is able, disrupts life's fellowship. For we cannot do everything by ourselves. One person is more useful in one matter, another in another matter. For that reason friendships [*amicitiae*] are formed – so that the common interest is maintained by mutual services.[46]

Present day social tastes may baulk at such a forthright treatment of the principle of exchange, the give-and-take or reciprocity that for us is normally an unspoken (but nonetheless inherent) indication of the trust underlying friendship. Martial and the ancient Romans, however, felt no compunction in speaking about what was fundamental to their society and arguably to its success as a world power – namely, the creation of trust and then the building of community that came through the process of exchange.[47] As Verboven puts it: '*Fides* was conceived [by the Romans] as crucial to the whole of social life... There was a *communis fides* owed to all mankind and a specific *fides* owed to fellow citizens' (2002, 40).

Like Cicero and Seneca, Martial also speaks of the workings and importance of *fides*:

> Callidus effracta nummos fur auferet arca,
>   prosternet patrios impia flamma lares:
> debitor usuram pariter sortemque negabit,
>   non reddet sterilis semina iacta seges:
> dispensatorem fallax spoliabit amica,
>   mercibus extructas abruet unda rates.
> extra fortunam est quidquid donatur amicis:
> quas dederis, solas semper habebis opes.

5.42

A cunning thief will break open and carry off the coins from your money chest; an unholy fire will lay low your ancestral home; a debtor will deny both interest and principal alike; the sterile soil will not give return on the sown seed; a deceptive mistress will rob your steward; a wave will overcome your ships piled up with merchandise. But beyond Fortune is whatever is given to friends: only that wealth which you have given away will you always have.

Unfortunately some readers compartmentalize this beautiful expression of the philosophy of reciprocity as an eloquent but cleverly couched solicitation for gifts and support.[48] With the last couplet of the poem, however, Martial goes to the very heart of social exchange and the workings of *amicitia*: a social bond or *fides* always begins with voluntary giving. Once *fides* has been established by the giving of a gift, your friends truly do become a source of imperishable wealth since they are socially obligated to reciprocate. For they represent the intangible benefits in gratitude and prestige that result from the goods and services regularly given in order to establish and maintain a friendship.

Epigram 5.42, then, is hardly a solicitation for gifts: rather it is a poetic statement of principles of social exchange and an enlightening glimpse into the workings and effects of ancient Roman friendship, as well as friendship in general.[49] It also describes a most valuable resource for an ancient Roman of the upper classes: a type of capital that was more flexible, honourable, prestigious, and lasting than material possessions.[50] As Blau put it in speaking of the modern day theory of social exchange: 'A man who helps others earns their gratitude and appreciation, and puts them into his debt, which promises to bring him further rewards in the future... Giving is, indeed, more blessed than receiving, for having social credit is preferable to being socially indebted.'[51]

In summation, to construe Martial as mercenary in his representation of friendship is to ignore or misinterpret the fundamental workings and results of friendship, as formulated by the theory of social exchange and specifically applied to ancient Roman friendship. The many poems Martial wrote on *amicitia* have the effect of reminding his reader of the high importance of social exchange and its importance to the community: for the regular exchange of goods and services is essential because through it one can establish trust and relationships, which in turn create strong social ties that make a social community function and prosper.

3

Poems of Praise

A certain person who was praised in my book, Faustinus, plays
innocent, as if he owed me nothing. He has cheated me!

Martial 5.36

Approximately twenty-seven per cent of the epigrams of Books 1-12
contain approval or praise of a person, or of their behaviour – another
point of similarity between Martial and the Indo-European poet-
singer, since praise, along with blame, was one of the major components of that tradition.[1] A few of these approbative poems comment on
historical figures of the past, but in most Martial addresses friends
and literary patrons, many of whom are historical persons from his
own time, although others are now only names.[2] Most frequently
Martial addresses the Emperor Domitian in this manner, under whom
he did most of his writing. Readers can be uncomfortable with, and
suspicious of, these poems of praise, particularly those on or to Domitian: they construe Martial's praise as flattery because of its frequency
and effusiveness, and thus take him as servile and mercenary because
of it.[3] As if in reaction, a number of readers and critics have assumed
a subversive subtext to explain Martial's excessive praise of an emperor who is generally assumed as bad: that is, they presume that
Martial's praise actually concealed criticism.[4]

These poems of praise can only be understood and appreciated,
however, within their social context. It will be argued below that they,
just as did his invective poems, catalogued social views and practices
but also in part had the effect of strengthening norms for his readership. More significantly, these poems of praise, just as with his poems
on friendship, have as their context the practice of reciprocity. They
thus had the effect of encouraging trust and social exchange, thereby
strengthening and unifying the social community. Also, Martial, with
his poems that honour the Emperor Domitian, represented a system
of political exchange that occurs between the emperor and the commu-

nity: where in exchange for legitimation of his position of power the emperor wields that power fairly and also gives back to the community in appropriate ways.

Praise poetry as social control

Poems of praise, although not normally as powerful as blame poems, which had more popular appeal and hence more potency, also had a strong influence on their audience.[5] For praise can be as much an instrument of influence and control as blame:[6] both could be used to describe and to some degree prescribe to their audiences the shared customs, morals, and ethics of the social group, thereby maintaining unity and giving direction. Moreover, compliments are more socially acceptable and thus not restricted to a specific context (as is invective). Indeed, because the praise poet sought to ennoble, uplift, and unify through the magnifying of his subject, he had more appeal to the wealthy and powerful – those who most sought praise and fame for their accomplishments.[7]

Given that poems of both blame and praise have the ability to influence and even control, much of what has been said of invective poetry in Chapter 1 will also apply to approbative poems. Indeed, Martial's poems of praise, like his poems of blame, were not just a personalized treatment of an individual but were also a poeticized (according to literary convention and the author's elaboration upon it) and idealized representation of their subject.[8] That representation of idealized behaviour had the effect of encouraging behaviour beneficial to the social community. For instance, at epigram 1.39 Martial praises his friend, Decianus, for his good character, culture, and learning:[9]

> Si quis erit raros inter numerandus amicos,
>   Quales prisca fides famaque novit anus,
> si quis Cecropiae madidus Latiaeque Minervae,
>   artibus et vera simplicitate bonus,
> si quis erit recti custos, mirator honesti,
>   et nuhil arcano qui roget ore deos,
> si quis erit magnae subnixus robore mentis:
>   dispeream si non hic Decianus erit.

1.39

If there is anyone to be numbered with such rare friends as old-time faith and ancient fame know of, one steeped in the arts of Cecropian and Latin Minerva, a good man, truly without guile; if there is anyone that guards the right, admires virtue, and asks nothing from the gods with inaudible voice; if there is anyone that relies on the strength of a noble heart: damn me if it isn't Decianus.

There is more to this poem than Martial showing his high regard for Decianus: for, although Decianus is presumed historical and could have been as Martial describes him here, the ideal in character whom Martial presents in this poem – called the *vir bonus*, the 'good man' – appears so frequently in various guises that it is thematic in his book collection.[10] Thus does Martial bring together in balance his desire to honour Decianus in an appropriate way and his own conception of good character.

Epigram 6.25 is another good example of Martial's facility as a poet to produce a poem that both praises on a personal level and communicates a behavioural ideal, too:

> Marcelline, boni suboles sincera parentis,
>   horrida Parrhasio quem tegit ursa iugo,
> ille vetus pro te patriusque quid optet amicus
>   accipe et haec memori pectore vota tene:
> cauta sit ut virtus, nec te temerarius ardor
>   in medios enses saevaque tela ferat.
> bella velint Martemque ferum rationis egentes;
>   tu potes et patris miles et esse ducis.

6.25

Marcellinus, true offspring of a good parent, whom the shaggy bear covers with its Parrhasion yoke, hear what that old friend of your father's wishes for you, and hold these prayers in a mindful heart: that cautious be your courage, and too rash an ardour not carry you into the midst of swords and cruel spears. Let those lacking rationality wish for wars and savage Mars. You can be both your father's soldier and your emperor's.

Here Martial gives praise to both Marcellinus and his father by the recognition he gives to Marcellinus' military service. With his warning to the young man not to get caught up in the insanity of war he at the same time highlights the family's zeal to serve and also keeps the addressee and reader mindful of the correct attitude towards war – that one must not get carried away by bloodlust.[11] Martial's inspired treatment is especially visible in the wonderfully expressive contrast he makes in the last line between being a soldier both for a father and for the emperor: the thought is that a parent would stress caution and self-preservation during battle while the emperor would reward bold courage and self-sacrifice. Martial's advice to Marcellinus (and his readers) is thus both personal and humane as well as public and civic-minded.

Others of Martial's poems of praise are more subtle in their combining of the personal with the ethical component in their laudatory representation of the honorand, alternately stressing one component more than the other and leaving the reader to draw the inference: for example, in several of his epigrams addressed to Aulus Pudens, who is portrayed elsewhere as a dear friend, Pudens is given little or no recognition or praise (beyond his mention) at the expense of Martial's point.[12] Obversely, at epigram 10.13, written in address of Manius, a childhood friend from Spain, Martial praises him at length, and lets his reader simply infer his general point – how valuable friendship can be. Yet, whatever the balance between the personal and ethical components in his representations of his honorands, Martial's poems of praise, just as his invective poems, reflect and even prescribe social values.

Reciprocity: you owe me

The main charge that critics brought against praise poets – the charge that is also regularly brought against Martial – is that their praise was only self-serving and mercenary flattery: in other words, that they had prostituted their literary skills.[13] Simonides, for example, often said to be the first professional poet, had a reputation for avarice and for being openly commercial in his relationship with those who commissioned his works.[14] Pindar, too, the best known and best represented praise poet from ancient Greek times, has been charged in both ancient and modern times with being mercenary: for example, the scholiasts and critics make inferences about his love for money when he praises wealth, or they sometimes see a hint at a request for payment in his poems.[15]

Yet Pindar's own representation of himself in his poems, which stands as a model for praise poets in general and for Martial, too, at least suggests that the true praise poet was not mercenary. To begin with, Pindar did not see his poetry as something he sold. Rather, he most often characterized himself (via his poet-persona) as a ξένος, a 'guest-friend', in his relationship with the person who had commissioned one of his poems; and as a guest-friend he was entertained and given gifts by his host, the victor, whom, upon his return home, he celebrated with his poem.[16] This was more than just an advertising ploy, for as Kurke, in her economically based treatment of Pindar's poetry, sees it, Pindar exemplified the so-called embedded form of economy – that is, the long-standing system of gift exchange, which was based on reciprocity and was embedded in community practices; this traditional embedded economy was for a time co-existing, somewhat uneasily, with the new system of money-based economy (a disembedded economy brought about by the invention of coinage), wherein individuals amassed wealth and power to the degree that they threatened the community (by their withdrawal from public life and service).[17] Kurke, in her reading of *Isthmian* 2.1-12, the passage on Pindar's so-called mercenary Muse (which, she maintains, is central to any account of Pindar's economics), argues that Pindar is teaching or re-educating his aristocratic audience for their place in the new economy – specifically, how they should utilize their wealth and resources in service of the social community.[18] Pindar's answer, then, to the charge that he was too concerned with money and return would be that in his talk of returns on his poetry he was actually teaching and guiding his addressee and audience in the proper use of their resources through his praise of the praiseworthy, and that he was doing this for their good and ultimately for the benefit of the entire community.[19]

Likewise, when Martial speaks of money or returns for his poems of praise, he too was reminding or instructing his audience that social exchange was necessary for the health and stability of the social community. More the blame poet than a praise poet (there is far more invective than praise in his twelve-book collection), Martial is able to speak openly about the reciprocity he expected from those he praised with his poems:

> Laudatus nostro quidam, Faustine, libello
> dissimulat, quasi nil debeat: imposuit.
>
> 5.36

> A certain person who was praised in my book, Faustinus, plays innocent, as if he owed me nothing. He has cheated me!

Martial here openly expresses the normally unexpressed underlying principle of reciprocity in human interaction or interpersonal relations – that return must be given for services granted. Of course Martial's poems on *amicitia* are shot through with this same exposition on the importance of social exchange.[20] Yet this plain speaking about the return he expects specifically from his poems of praise has given the impression to many readers that Martial was both insincere and mercenary in his poems of praise.[21] This, however, is an unfair judgment. In the first place, Martial was entitled to remuneration for the service he performed as a praise poet. That he states this is not out of line – for instance, Seneca himself in his essay on *beneficia* advises that those who confer benefits on others sometimes should prompt the recipient to make proper return:

> When we say that it is not proper to ask for reciprocation of a benefit, we don't in every case exclude the request for return. For often bad people need a debt collector, and good people a reminder.
> *de Ben.* 7.23.3

Moreover, as one who represents and writes for his social community, Martial is permitted forthright expression in order to address community-wide problems, which is just what he does with epigram 5.36: that is, he addresses the problem of a general ignorance or disregard for the process of exchange that was so vital to society's health. For not only does Martial treat the topic several times (e.g. at epigrams 5.15 and 5.19), but so do his contemporaries, Pliny and Juvenal.[22] Pliny, for example, in his eulogy of Martial (*Ep.* 3.21) complains that people no longer follow the old custom (*mos antiquus*) of rewarding poets who praise individuals or cities with either honours or money. Pliny tells us that he, on the other hand, showed his gratitude for the verses Martial wrote of him (see Martial 10.20) by giving Martial money to make his trip back to Spain. Of course Martial, Pliny, and Juvenal see and treat this problem of lack of proper return through the eyes of a writer. Yet the underlying issue here is the same issue targeted by Seneca in his *de Beneficiis*: namely, *ingratia*, 'ingratitude', which, as Seneca puts it, is the worst of all crimes: for without proper return for *beneficia*, 'favours', the social community will not hold together (*de Ben.* 1.4.2). Martial likewise is pointing up this ethic with epigram 5.36 rather than making a specific and socially inappropriate request for return on his poetry.

In another poem Martial speaks again on the issue of return for his service as a poet and reveals even more of this ethic of reciprocity that forms the context for his poems of praise:

> Quintus nostrorum liber est, Auguste, iocorum
>   et queritur laesus carmine nemo meo,
> gaudet honorato sed multus nomine lector,
>   cui victura meo munere fama datur.
> 'quid tamen haec prosunt quamvis venerantia multos?'
>   non prosint sane, me tamen ista iuvant.

5.15

This is the fifth book of my jokes, Augustus, and no one complains that he has been harmed by my poems. Rather, many a reader is pleased by his name being honoured since enduring fame is given to him through my gift. 'But what profit do these poems bring even though they honour many?' Although they certainly bring no profit, nevertheless they please me.

Readers may be tempted to take this poem only as a plea for material support from readers and especially from the emperor – as if Martial were saying: 'Poor me; see how I can't get proper return on my poetry – especially from the ones who really owe me for my praise of them; and though I'm downplaying my disappointment, I'm really asking for your support, Domitian.'[23] Yet, the effect of the poem is to remind Martial's readers that there is a system of exchange inherent in human relationships that must not be ignored. Specifically, much as Pindar instructed his addressees and audience on the proper use of wealth for their benefit and the benefit of the community, Martial with this poem reminds the wealthy and accomplished individuals whom he honours with his poems to do their part in social and political life – that is, to use their resources to build and maintain the social community rather than withdraw and just amass wealth for personal interests.[24]

Moreover, Martial actually does reap a type of return with this poem – one that is part of the process of social exchange: namely, by informing the social community that he provides a service to it *gratis* he increases his personal status. For in the process of social exchange if the recipient of the benefit or gift does not respond in kind, the giver gains status while the unresponsive recipient loses status.[25] Blau gives a simple and lucid explanation of this type of exchange:

> A person who gives others valuable gifts or renders them important services makes a claim for superior status by obligating them to himself. If they return benefits that adequately discharge their obligations, they deny his claim to superiority, and if their returns are excessive, they make a counterclaim to superiority over him. If they fail to reciprocate with benefits that are at least as important to him as his are to them, they validate his claim to superiority over him.
>
> 1964, 108

As applied here in this epigram (5.15), Martial has established superiority over the unnamed persons he has praised in his poems, since they have not reciprocated in kind. These persons, and those like them, lose credit and trust, and in the future will be excluded from exchanges; also their social status will decline as their reputation for not honouring their social debts spreads through the community.[26] The poet's status, on the other hand, has increased in proportion because of his willingness to attempt an exchange, which is the beginning of the process of establishing trust and building community.[27] To put it another way, Martial gets bragging rights in return for his poems of praise that have gone unreciprocated: he is able to boast to the emperor, no less, about the service he supplies to the social community for no reward except his own pleasure; thus does he build his reputation and increase his status within that social community.[28] This is a palpable return because it wins him the respect, approval, and affection of his friends, as well as of the one person who could best make proper return for Martial's services to the social community – the emperor.[29]

Martial's petitions to Domitian: secondary exchange

Over ninety poems and a few prose epistles, which comprise approximately eight per cent of the total of 1,174 epigrams in Books 1-12, contain express praise or approval of the reigning emperor, thus making the emperor Martial's most frequent honorand.[30] Most of these poems or prose epistles are addressed to, or largely concern, the Emperor Domitian – seventy-six altogether.[31] These poems, like the larger group of approbative poems or prose epistles of which they are a part, are poeticized treatments of their subject with social exchange or reciprocity as their underlying premise: they serve as Martial's currency in the process of social exchange. Likewise these poems on the emperor have the effect of instructing and guiding his social community on the importance of social exchange. Yet, since the emperor has a uniquely high degree of power and autonomy, Martial's dialogue with him will be shown to involve another type of exchange as well – namely, where Martial plays the role of power broker between the emperor and the social community.

Epigram 2.91 illustrates well that social exchange is still the basis of Martial's poems of praise of Domitian, but is also the first half of an exchange between poet and emperor that reveals the full significance of Martial's addresses to, or representations of, the emperor:

Rerum certa salus, terrarum gloria, Caesar,
   sospite quo magnos credimus esse deos,
si festinatis totiens collecta libellis
   detinuere oculos carmina nostra tuos,
quod fortuna vetet fieri, permitte videri,
   natorum genitor credar ut esse trium.
haec, si displicui, fuerint solacia nobis;
   haec fuerint nobis praemia, si placui.

2.91

> Caesar, certain defender of the world, glory of the earth, through whose well-being we have faith that the great gods exist, if my poems, so often collected in hasty little books, have detained your eyes, what fortune forbids to be, permit that it seem so: that I may be taken for the father of three. If I have displeased, let this be my consolation; this my reward if I have pleased.

Here the poet, although not in actuality a father of three, petitions Domitian for the *ius trium liberorum*, the right of three children, a high honour which granted certain privileges to its holders – the right to inherit, for example.[32] The poet asks this right in exchange for any pleasure his poems have brought to the emperor. The poem's basis in the principle of social exchange is obvious, but closer scrutiny shows a playful and poetical blend of half-truths that gives the poem more effect than as a simple illustration of reciprocity.[33] For what Martial has created here is a poeticized version of a formal petition (also termed a *libellus*) that turns out to be the set-up for a joke in the next epigram, 2.92.[34] There the poet tells his reader that he who alone had the power – that is, the emperor – has granted his petition for the right of three children; then he bids his wife goodbye (i.e. he divorces her) because 'our Lord's gift ought not to be wasted' (2.92.4). Thus is Martial able with the two epigrams, with his fabricated version of a formal petition, to give recognition to the emperor's generosity in a humorous and entertaining way.[35]

What, then, is the intention and effect of Martial's poeticized and humorous account of his receiving this high honour from Domitian? At the basic level, as with other of Martial's poems that speak of reciprocity, there is the underlying reminder to his reader about the reciprocity inherent in all interpersonal relations – a reciprocity that is necessary to a unified social community. Of course, Martial's addressing the emperor gives his remarks all the more weight, for it implies that even Domitian himself was part of the social community created through social exchange.[36] It is as if Martial were boasting to his reader with his cycle of poems on the right of three children: 'Look how the emperor himself has engaged in social exchange with me, the humble poet.'[37]

Yet Martial's representation of the exchange between poet and emperor, as exampled here in 2.91, has additional significance. Poems that are premised on a social exchange between the poet and the emperor are distinguished from Martial's poems of praise for non-imperial friends and patrons by the social and political right of the poet to seek and engage in exchange with the emperor. That is shown in epigrams 2.91 and 2.92 by the poet being represented as receiving the right of three children, whether or not his poems had pleased the emperor: simply his asking in a respectful and reverent way seemed to have entitled him to it. Other poems also present this right, always in a respectful and laudatory manner. For example, in epigram 8.82, where Martial again draws a parallel between formal prose petitions and his own poems to the emperor, his phrasing of the poet's right to petition the emperor sounds almost as if it were a prayer: he asks Domitian to bear with his poets, for they are his 'sweet glory', and then he enjoins him to allow that their 'civic crown of ivy' also to be made for him, along with the civic and military crowns he has received.[38] The poem, however, that best reveals the social and political sense of Martial's representation of the right to petition the emperor is 8.24:

> Si quid forte petam timido gracilique libello,
>   improba non fuerit si mea charta, dato.
> et si non dederis, Caesar, permitte rogari:
>   offendunt numquam tura precesque Iovem.
> qui fingit sacros auro vel marmore vultus,
>   non facit ille deos: qui rogat, ille facit.

8.24

If by chance I petition for something in my timid and slight book, if my page is not improper, then grant it. And if you do not grant it, Caesar, allow yourself to be asked. Incense and prayers never offend Jupiter. The person who makes sacred images in gold or marble does not make gods: he who asks of them makes them gods.

Martial here has his persona justify, in a laudatory fashion, the petition format he uses (e.g. at 2.91) in his requests of the emperor for goods or services.[39] He predicates his right to petition on the analogy that it is prayers that make a god, and not simply honoraria in the form of statues: thus does he cleverly combine justification for his

63

requests with high praise of the emperor – that is, his likening of him to Jupiter.[40]

Imbedded in this justification in epigram 8.24 for Martial's petitions to the emperor is another type of exchange inherent in all of Martial's poems to or on the emperor: in exchange for a respectful acknowledgment, via poems, of the emperor's power, the emperor makes responsible use of his great power by being accessible and responsive to the petitions of both poets and people in general.[41] Indeed, this topic of the emperor making proper return to his subjects – *euergetism*, as termed by Veyne, which is the giving of 'bread and circuses' as well as temples and other buildings, was very dear to Martial: for he makes it his most frequent theme in his poems on Domitian.[42] As Nauta, in his study of poets and patrons during the time of Domitian, characterizes the nature of this imperial exchange process of *euergetism* (2002, 387):

> the emperor deployed his superior resources to please his subjects, and the subjects honoured and exalted their emperor.

Nauta then goes on to define this relationship as 'community patronage' between the emperor, as patron, and his subjects, as the clients – which was a reflection of the 'personal patronage' between Martial and Domitian.[43] In fact, this community patronage Nauta speaks of has a history: Augustus instituted just such a patronal relationship between emperor and subject in order to help establish and legitimate his own position as emperor, and this ideology of the good emperor as a paternal protector and benefactor continued through Martial's times.[44]

This type of patronal relationship between the emperor and his subjects has an analogue in the socio-anthropological model of exchange theory that can serve as an objective test for validity.[45] According to exchange theory, whenever power is collected in the hands of a single person, or a few, a secondary exchange is superimposed upon the primary exchange of goods and services (reciprocity in interpersonal relations).[46] In this secondary exchange the group or person in power, the emperor in Martial's case, offers fairness in the exercise of power in exchange for the collective approval and support – called legitimation – from those immediately subject to his power, namely, in this case, most immediately, the upper classes, but also the plebeians. The distinctive characteristic of authority thus legitimated is that a superior's commands are obeyed not because of his or her sanctioning power, but because of the normative pressure exercised among the subordinates themselves, particularly once these normative constraints have become institutionalized. For instance, in Martial's era the upper classes had legitimated the emperor's authority by having made the great power and autonomy entrusted to the emperor a part of their own social and political ideology. This legitimation process had begun as far back as Augustus' reign, and by Martial's time the Roman upper classes (and plebeians) had long since incorporated the concept of an all-powerful leader into their political ideology – even the senatorial source Tacitus attests to this.[47]

The application of this socio-anthropological model of secondary exchange to Martial's poems of praise reveals something quite contrary to the usual perception. For readers have generally viewed Martial as giving the emperor any praise he wants or allows – no matter how remote from the truth that might be – in order to get some return from him or, at least, to stay in his favour so that he can continue to write. In other words, they view Martial as subjugating his integrity and his gift as a poet to Domitian's power and ego in order to further his personal interests in some way. A good illustration of this is Martial's use of the title *dominus deusque*, 'lord and god', for Domitian, which, in a poem written after Domitian's assassination, he (via his poet-persona) declares he will not use of Trajan.[48] Thus does he give the impression that he used it unwillingly of Domitian. Martial's emphasis, however, on the power and control of the petitioner in epigram 8.24 helps put the perception of his interaction with the emperor back into proper balance. He is subjugated to the emperor in just the degree the emperor is subjugated to him – or to him and his constituency, rather, who are his readers.[49] For Martial – as the representative of his readers – and the emperor are symbiotic partners in the ongoing process of negotiation and exchange between the two: namely, where the emperor plays a role similar to that of a patron to his client subjects. Only if he plays his patronal role well, does he get collective approval and support – legitimation – from his client-subjects.

That Martial's legitimation of Domitian via his poems of praise was their underlying purpose is made even more obvious by Domitian's violation of the unwritten contract that was the basis of the exchange between the emperor and his subjects. For, when Domitian in the later part of his reign did indeed get so bad, when in particular his relationship with the Senate and especially with those nearest to him deteriorated so that he trusted no one and no one could trust him, he was assassinated and through senatorial *damnatio* was denied even posthumous legitimation.[50] Martial reflects this breach of trust between the emperor and his subjects in a poem intended to legitimate Domitian's senatorially appointed successor, Nerva:

> Quae modo litoreos ibatis carmina Pyrgos,
>   ite Sacra, iam non pulverulenta, via.
> contigit Ausoniae procerum mitissimus aulae
>   Nerva: licet tuto nunc Helicone frui:
> recta fides, hilaris clementia, cauta potestas
>   iam redeunt; longi terga dedere metus.
> hoc populi gentesque tuae, pia Roma, precantur:
>   dux tibi sit semper talis, et iste diu.

12.5

You poems that were lately on your way to Pyrgi on the sea, go on the Sacred Way, no longer dusty. The mildest of nobles, Nerva, has arrived at the Ausonian palace. Now it's possible to enjoy a safe Helicon. Honest trust, cheerful clemency, restrained power now return. Longstanding fear has taken flight. Dutiful Rome, your peoples and nations pray this: may your leader always be such as he, and for a long time.

Throughout much of the poem Martial contrasts Nerva with his assassinated predecessor, Domitian: Nerva is mild, Domitian was severe; in Domitian's reign Rome faced distrust and intrigue, cruelty, abuse of power, and terror, whereas under Nerva good and easy relations have returned; all of this strongly implies that the trust that was necessary for a healthy exchange between emperor and subjects had deteriorated under Domitian.[51] Martial then ends the poem by instructing the dutiful or loyal citizens (*pia Roma*) to honour their new emperor, thus doing his part to legitimate Nerva.

In another epigram, wherein he legitimates Trajan, Nerva's successor, Martial again reveals how Domitian breached the unwritten agreement he had with the social community:

Frustra, Blanditiae, venitis ad me
attritis miserabiles labellis:
dicturus dominum deumque non sum.
iam non est locus hac in urbe vobis;
ad Parthos procul ite pilleatos
et turpes humilesque supplicesque
pictorum sola basiate regum.
non est hic dominus, sed imperator,
sed iustissimus omnium senator,
per quem de Stygia domo reducta est
siccis rustica Veritas capillis.
hoc sub principe, si sapis, caveto
verbis, Roma, prioribus loquaris.

10.72

In vain, Flatteries, you have come to me, miserable with your shameless lips. I am not going to say 'lord and god'. Now there is no place for you in this city. Go far off to felt-capped Parthians and as base and lowly supplicants kiss the feet of embroidered kings. Not here is there a lord, but a commander-in-chief, the most just senator of all, under whom unadorned and rustic Truth has been brought back from the Stygian house. Under this ruler, if you are wise, beware, Rome, of speaking with words from prior times.

Martial focuses here on Domitian's abuse of the imperial cult – specifically, his arrogance in equating himself with a god by either requiring or allowing the title *dominus deusque*, 'lord and god', in official correspondence at Rome as well as in letters and other formats.[52] The imperial cult was a particularly sensitive area of concern for the emperor and the upper classes, for it involved negotiation and exchange between the emperor and his subjects and thus was a highly visible and telling part of the overall process of legitimation. As Nauta expresses it:

The imperial cult, like patronage, was a question of negotiation, in which both parties made moves in order to define their relationship... [E]lite opinion at Rome kept a close and suspicious watch on how the emperor conducted these negotiations. Too uninhibited a divinisation was not appreciated, because it was a sign of arrogance and loss of perspective ...'[53]

Should the emperor overstep the accepted bounds in allowing or even requiring (as did Caligula, for example) that he be allowed, while alive, divine status at Rome, it marked him as arrogant and, as Martial's image in this poem of shunting the practice to the East implies, stigmatized him for assuming the intolerable status of tyrant or king at Rome.[54]

Martial as power broker

Given that the process of secondary exchange and legitimation underlies Martial's poems on the emperor, how, then, should one take his supposed and self-admitted flattery of Domitian? Perhaps the best way to understand the intention and effect of Martial's praise of the emperors is to see him as a mediator or broker in the legitimation process that was ongoing between the emperor and the social community. As a broker he tried to represent – using a literary format and its traditions – both parties in a positive and non-antagonistic way so that the dialogue continued successfully and the social community remained stable and productive. This was especially difficult to do since imperial policies and political conditions changed from one emperor to the next, and sometimes from one day to the next. Also it was difficult because of the usually fragile relationship between the emperor and upper classes – particularly the senators – due in good part to the perception that the emperor was in principle no more than a senator with special powers and honours granted him by the senate and people.[55] Thus Martial could be expected to err in his representation of emperor and upper classes alike in these highly complex negotiations. That he managed to represent them so successfully for so long under such a difficult emperor as Domitian shows both his good faith (i.e. sincerity) and great skill.

To continue with the analogy, as a broker Martial worked for both sides impartially, trying to represent each to best advantage, but owing allegiance above all to the social community they together comprised. For example, in order to accommodate Domitian, Martial several times cut back on the obscenity and sexual content in his books, apparently out of deference for Domitian's programme for moral reform (Books 5 and 8).[56] In doing this he legitimated Domitian by espousing imperial policy, replete with an unblemished portrait of Domitian's own questionable morality.[57] Also in doing so he reflected and probably in part prescribed the loyalty and support the social community felt or should feel for Domitian. Moreover, in this legitimation process Martial's praise of the emperor was generally moderate and tasteful when considered in the context of the tradition of imperial panegyric – a tradition that had common motifs, such as the claim that the times of the current emperor were superior to earlier times (e.g. at epigram 5.19.1-2), and which tradition also from Julius Caesar's time included some form of divinization.[58] Yet, on the other hand, in order to accommodate the social community, in his other books Martial justified and used obscenity and sexual material liberally with the awareness that they were an expression of his readers' subconscious or primal instincts and feelings that was necessary to the health and growth of the social community.[59] Again, in its context his use of obscenity and sexual content was tastefully done, with many a disclaimer to preclude offence and antagonism.[60]

Considered in this context, Martial's praise of Domitian, even though it may well have proven inaccurate historically, was entirely sincere and even truthful in that it defined the perception of the emperor that his readership held, if not always the emperor himself.[61] Such a perception was partly determined by Domitian's individualistic character, vision, and methods of governing, which the social community would have to accommodate to a degree, even if these were repugnant to some of them, but this perception was also very much determined by both traditional and contemporary standards of behaviour for an emperor.[62] In other words, although Martial did tailor his epigrams to fit Domitian specifically – for example, with his praise of Domitian's military accomplishments, building programme, and moral reforms – over and above that he was giving expression and definition to a perception of what the Roman Empire, as represented by the emperor, was and should be.[63]

Moreover, any type of subversive subtext clearly would not fit in with Martial's partly descriptive and partly proscriptive representation of the emperor in his poems.[64] For not only would it undermine the process of legitimation that the court poets regularly performed for the emperors through their imperial panegyric, but it would also taint all other poems of praise (i.e. with non-imperial honorands).[65] In addition, a subversive subtext simply does not accord with what was normally the method and purpose of a poet working in the iambic tradition – that is, a poet who represented the ethics of the social community. For the iambic poet delivered both blame and praise in a candid and sincere fashion, with no subtext intended or needed, for that matter, since the poet was already speaking in a forthright manner that had social and religious sanction.[66] In other words, for Martial to criticize Domitian, he would have to have had communal sanction for it – as he did after Domitian's assassination; and when he did do it, he would have done it in a candid manner (as he did).[67]

As for Martial's self-admitted flattery of Domitian at epigram 10.72 (see above) and derogatory remarks directed at him in retrospect (see at epigram 12.5 above), these can be explained or justified in two ways. First, they are spoken as a part of hindsight, when Domitian's transgressions as emperor were on public record for the community. As Coleman perceptively states it, since the Flavian regime and its value-system had been so long established at the time of Domitian's assassination (more than twenty-five years), the broad spectrum of the population of Rome, including Martial, would have been unaware of the military, financial, and political problems and disturbances that came towards the end of Domitian's reign (1998, 354). This makes more sense since Domitian was not consistently bad in his governing: instead the overall record shows him as efficient and effective in some areas, while lacking fatally (as it turned out) in others.[68] Thus, he would have been as difficult to assess back then as he is for historians now.[69]

The second explanation or justification for Martial's confession of flattering Domitian and his other derogatory remarks is that they are part of the process of the legitimation of a new emperor (Nerva and then Trajan), and thus are tailored to fit the character, vision, and methods of governing of that emperor. For example, Trajan, as reflected in Pliny's *Panegyricus*, instituted a new policy on imperial panegyric that rejected the blatant flattery (*adulatio*), which had been encouraged by Domitian, for 'a "true" *laudatio* based on the virtues and accomplishments of the ruling *princeps*'.[70] In light of this, Martial's renunciation of *blanditiae* at epigram 10.72 was not meant so much as a condemnation of Domitian's encouragement of flattery as a show of support – and hence part of the legitimation process – for Trajan and his new policy. Likewise Martial's comment that Domitian was a 'harsh *princeps*' who ruled in 'evil times' (12.3.11-12) was meant to point up the mildness of Nerva (12.5.3), as well as his trustworthiness, clemency, and cautious use of his power (12.5.5).[71] Martial's condemnations of Domitian, then, were just one of the traditional ways to praise and legitimate the current emperor.[72]

4

The Good Life

Great king of ancient heavens and a former world, under whom
was a lazy repose, not any labour, nor too regal a thunderbolt,
nor any deserving of a thunderbolt, nor was the ground cut to the
spirit world, but its riches were kept to itself: come, joyful and
obliging, to the yearly delights of Priscus. It is fitting that you be
with your rites.

Martial 12.62.1-6

Martial does most of his philosophizing indirectly through his invective and poems of praise – highly palatable delivery devices for a
system of ethics that have fooled more than one respectable critic into
thinking they were only meant to entertain or simply flatter.[1] Yet in
addition to this piecemeal delivery of mostly an ethical philosophy,
Martial occasionally presents a more comprehensive and unifying
expression of what he considers to be the best type of life. He does this
through twenty-five poems, most of which have at their heart a
pastoral ideal – a primitivistic conception of life in the country that is
grounded in the ancient Roman archetype of a mythical golden age
associated with the reign of Saturn.[2]

This primitivistic world view that Martial uses in his poems on the
good life is meant to address the seemingly inevitable ills that attend
a complex and civilized society – specifically, the sometimes mindless
and despiritualizing constraints that society imposes on the individual, and also the excessive labour which society necessitates in order
to attain what is considered adequate for a civilized existence. Martial,
in opposition to a degrading and unnecessarily arduous way of living
that he reckons as a waste of life, counterposes a vision of a golden age
existence: a return to humankind's primeval and communal state
during the reign of Saturn.

The urban-rural antithesis

The most striking aspect of Martial's philosophy of life as presented in his poetry is the radical lifestyle he seems to advocate: he seemingly would have his readers relax their ambitions for money, power, and glory – the traditional markers of success for ancient Romans – in order to spend their time at leisure in a more natural type of existence. He gives strong and characteristic expression to this alternative lifestyle in a poem addressed to the very accomplished, highly respected, and best known teacher and academician of his time, Quintilian:

> Quintiliane, vagae moderator summe iuventae,
>   gloria Romanae, Quintiliane, togae,
> vivere quod propero pauper nec inutilis annis,
>   da veniam: properat vivere nemo satis.
> differat hoc patrios optat qui vincere census
>   atriaque immodicis artat imaginibus.
> me focus et nigros non indignantia fumos
>   tecta iuvant et fons vivus et herba rudis.
> sit mihi verna satur, sit non doctissima coniunx,
>   sit nox cum somno, sit sine lite dies.

2.90

Quintilian, supreme restrainer of flighty youth, Quintilian, glory of the Roman toga, give pardon that I, a poor man not incapacitated by years, hasten to live: no one hastens to live enough. Let him put it off who desires to surpass his father's worth and cram his halls with too many portraits. A hearth and ceiling not resentful of black smoke please me, as also do a natural spring and uncultivated grass. Let me have a satisfied home-bred slave, a wife not too learned, a night with sleep and a day without lawsuit.

Martial sets up the poem by asking the illustrious Quintilian's pardon because his poet-persona, although not wealthy or incapacitated by age, hastens 'to live', *vivere*, an expression Martial uses many times to denote living life to its fullest – his own variation of the Horatian *carpe diem* motif.[3] Martial's contrast to this idea of living life to its fullest is a lifestyle driven by the ambition to amass glory and wealth – specifically in this case, striving for more wealth than one's father's – and by the immoderate desire to attain power and glory, as indicated with the image of an excessive number of *imagines*, wax portrait-masks of ancestors, jamming the halls of the home (5-6).[4] Martial counters this lifestyle that is driven by immoderate ambition with a relaxed, simplistic, and unpretentious style of life. The overall effect of this contrast is to bring the reader to the realization of what the proper balance is between one's personal desires and comfort, on the one hand, and the expectations and approval of society and family, on the other.

At the heart of this contrast between personal desires and societal expectations is the antithesis of an urban and rural existence – a standard antithesis for the ancient Romans and one which Martial regularly employed.[5] For example, in epigram 2.90 societal expectations are signified by the image of the person who wishes to amass money, power, and glory to an immoderate degree; and of course the normal setting for this was the city, where the bulk of the business of the market and government took place.[6] Then, as the corrective counter to this type of existence Martial uses a series of images in the rest of the poem, all of which at least suggest an ideal rural existence with their more natural setting. Specifically, his first image, a functional hearth that causes blackened ceilings, which is a topos for the simple country life, is contrasted to hearths in the atria of the wealthy, which were not used because of the damage the smoke would cause to the statues and panelled ceilings.[7] As for the significance of the imagery, the functioning hearth connotes an honesty or genuineness and emphasis on personal comfort as opposed to the stricture, artificiality, and coldness of a functional but unused hearth.[8] His second image, water from a natural stream and real grass, of course typical of a rural setting, is opposed to the piped in and sometimes impure water typical of the city, and the efforts of city dwellers to imitate a rural landscape.[9] The significance: again the stream and grass connote a genuineness and healthy naturalness in contrast to the artificiality and health risks typical of the city. The image of a home-bred and contented slave again conjures up a rural existence, and this is opposed to foreign slaves bought *en masse* as commodities just to have in order to impress – an extravagance typical of the city.[10] The wish for a wife not *doctissima*, 'too learned/cultured', juxtaposes the stereotype

of the domestically oriented and properly submissive woman with one
who would outdo her husband in education and culture, and hence
make his life difficult either with her ambitions or with her overshad-
owing of him.[11] Of course learning and culture are typically associated
with the city – especially since they are typically associated with the
wealthy – while Martial's ideal woman suggests the simple and natural, as typical of the country. Martial's final images, a night without
sleep and a day without a lawsuit, once again juxtapose the stressful
lifestyle typical of the high-achiever in the city with the natural,
relaxed, and leisurely pace of the country.

In other poems Martial expands on this urban-rural antithesis. For
example, in epigram 1.55 he uses the urban-rural contrast in present-
ing his ideal life: an existence on a modest but self-sustaining country
estate of his own.[12]

> Vota tui breviter si vis cognoscere Marci,
>   clarum militiae, Fronto, togaeque decus,
> hoc petit, esse sui nec magni ruris arator,
>   sordidaque in parvis otia rebus amat.
> quisquam picta colit Spartani frigora saxi
>   et matutinum portat ineptus have,
> cui licet exuviis nemoris rurisque beato
>   ante focum plenas explicuisse plagas
> et piscem tremula salientem ducere saeta
>   flavaque de rubro promere mella cado?
> pinguis inaequales onerat cui vilica mensas
>   et sua non emptus praeparat ova cinis?
> non amet hanc vitam quisquis me non amat, opto,
>   vivat et urbanis albus in officiis.

1.55

If you want to know in brief the prayers of your Marcus, Fronto
– renowned glory of the military and the toga – he seeks this: to
be the plougher of a his own farm, not large. He loves a rough
leisure in modest circumstances. Is anyone foolish enough to pay
court to the painted chill of Spartan stone and convey morning
greetings when it's possible for him, happy man, to open up nets
full with the spoils of the woods and countryside in front of the

fireplace, and to pull in the leaping fish with trembling line, and to take out yellow honey from a ruddy jar? If his bailiff's plump wife loads the crooked table and unbought charcoal cooks the eggs he owns? I wish that anyone who does not love me not love such a life, and that he live, pale, among the obligations of the city.

First and foremost the poet seeks the independence and leisure that productive land of his own will give him. Both of these, independence and leisure, are key components of Martial's concept of the ideal life, and are presented, as usual, in contrast to having to make a living by daily attendance at the atria for the early morning salutation – Martial's most frequent complaint about living in the city.[13] For the rural setting typically provides sustenance in plenty – something Martial regularly emphasizes, as he does here with several rich images of food – along with a hearth and firewood to cook it. Finally, as he concludes, life in the country is healthier than in the city, as suggested here by the paleness of the city-dweller.[14]

What is not mentioned in this otherwise typical urban-rural antithesis that Martial presents in epigram 1.55 is the ethical or moral condition of the city as opposed to the country. Another epigram, 4.5, well typifies this particular aspect of the city and country:

> Vir bonus et pauper linguaque et pectore verus,
> quid tibi vis, urbem qui, Fabiane, petis?
> qui nec leno potes nec comissator haberi,
> nec pavidos tristi voce citare reos,
> nec potes uxorem cari corrumpere amici,
> nec potes algentes arrigere ad vetulas,
> vendere nec vanos circa Palatia fumos,
> plaudere nec Cano, plaudere nec Glaphyro;
> unde miser vives? 'homo certus, fidus amicus' –
> hoc nihil est: numquam sic Philomelus eris

4.5

A good man and a poor one, true in tongue and heart, what are you wanting that you seek the city, Fabianus? You are not able to play the part of a pimp or a professional partygoer, nor to summon a trembling defendant with a stern voice. Nor are you able to seduce the wife of a dear friend, nor are you able to erect for cold old hags, or to sell empty smoke around the palace, or applaud Canus or applaud Glaphyrus.[15] How will you live, you unhappy man? 'A dependable person, a true friend' – this is nothing! You'll never be a Philomelus that way.[16]

According to Martial, the only way Fabianus, a rustic who is a good man (*vir bonus*), although not moneyed, will make good in the city is to do something either dishonest or dishonourable.[17] Even his dependability and faithfulness, qualities which served him well in the country and should have at least given him a fair chance at a livelihood and advancement through the social exchange system that was the basis of *amicitia*, count for nothing because of the duplicity and greed in the city.[18]

As these few examples serve to indicate, Martial typically with his urban-rural antithesis shows city life as difficult, dangerous, unhealthy, and immoral.[19] One lives in material want there because making an adequate living is so difficult, not only because the competition is fierce, but also because people often use dishonest and dishonourable means. All twelve books of Martial's collection are full of invective that hammers on the material and moral ills that are typical of the city. These poems especially focus on examples of avarice and extravagance, which drive the highly competitive and immoral nature of the urban lifestyle.[20] More specifically, people spurred by their immoderate desire for money and power use any means available to get all they can, thus making it difficult for others with moderate ambitions and scruples to make an honest living.[21]

That Martial should single out immoderate ambition for money, power, and glory as a general theme is neither unique nor surprising: the desire for money and power carried to excess was, to judge from the consistent condemnation of it in the literature, endemic among ancient Romans of the late Republic and Imperial periods.[22] Coming from humble beginnings to the level of a superpower in a relatively short time, the upper class Romans of the late Republic and early Imperial times had an ongoing struggle with their ambitions: on the one hand, the drive to achieve was the quality or characteristic that motivated them to accomplish so much; on the other hand, when ambition became immoderate and used dishonourable means to achieve results, it was a socially and personally destructive force.[23]

4. The Good Life

Sallust, in his account of Rome's remarkable rise to power, details the great struggle that the Romans had with controlling their ambitions (*Cat.* 7). In describing the Romans' early history he says that after they had changed from a monarchy to a republic, ruled by consuls and the Senate, the free state, once liberty was achieved, grew incredibly strong in a remarkably short time because the *cupido gloriae*, the 'desire for glory', had become so great (*Cat.* 7.1-3). Sallust explains that while the Romans were attaining their superpower status they desired glory only for their service to the state and wanted only 'honest wealth' (*divitias honestas*) – that is, wealth that had been acquired by honourable means (*Cat.* 7.4-6). Yet after Rome had grown great, when Carthage had been completely devastated by them (in 146 BCE), Sallust complains that they who had accomplished so much found their newly attained leisure and wealth to be a burden and misery. In Sallust's own words:

> For first the lust for power [(*cupido*) *imperi*] and then the lust for money [*cupido pecuniae*] grew. These were the substance, as it were, of all evils. For greed [*avaritia*] destroyed trust, integrity, and other noble qualities, and in their place taught arrogance, cruelty, neglect of the gods, and the setting of a price on everything. Ambition [*ambitio*] drove many people to become false: to have one thing shut up in their hearts and another ready on their tongue; to value friendships and enmities not on their merits but according to advantage; and to show a good face rather than a good character. At first these vices grew slowly and were punished on occasion. After, when the contagion had spread like a plague, the state was changed, and a government that was most just and best became cruel and intolerable.
>
> *Cat.* 10

Thus, as Sallust sees it, a lust for money, which he usually terms *avaritia*, and also a lust for power – *ambitio* in its negative sense – were the main Roman evils and were responsible for the degradation of the Roman state.[24] In fact, one could argue that immoderate desire for money and power was a social or cultural weakness endemic to the ancient Romans – the dark and destructive side to their unique gift, which was their penchant for establishing a hierarchical order.[25] It is

79

this immoderate ambition and its effects that Martial also focuses upon so often.

Sallust targets one other often found Roman vice that is tied closely to excessive ambition and desire, and this vice must be mentioned in order to appreciate fully Martial's representation of the good life. In speaking of Catiline's corrupt character Sallust maintains that it was spurred on by the corruption of the morals of the state, morals which were being shattered by two most pernicious evils of a diverse nature, *luxuria*, 'extravagance', and *avaritia*, 'greed' (*Cat.* 5.6-8). The link between *luxuria* and *avaritia*, besides that they both had to do with material wealth, is, as Sallust with much indignation states, that wealth acquired by dishonourable means seems to have been a plaything (*ludibrium*) to its possessor because it was squandered so shamelessly. The perception of wealth as a plaything then spurred, in turn, the strong desire (*lubido*) for lewdness, gluttony, and attendant vices. As examples of this *lubido* Sallust lists men playing the part of women; the scouring of land and sea in order to satisfy gluttony; and, as he sums it up, any reckless self-indulgence of the senses. This extravagance in turn initiated a vicious cycle of the re-acquisition of wealth by any means and then again the reckless and shameless waste of it (*Cat.* 13). Through this cycle the character flaw of extravagance, *luxuria*, was linked closely to *avaritia*. Of course, Martial also frequently targeted *luxuria* and its many attendant vices in his poems.

This bit of Roman moral history *à la* Sallust serves as a backdrop for Martial's invective, but also for his poems on the good life. For example, one can better understand what Martial intended in epigram 2.90 by asking one of the most gifted and accomplished public figures of his time to forgive him (his poet-persona) because he 'hastens to live' instead of strictly pursuing the traditional markers of success – money, power, and glory.[26] It is to this endemic and immoderate ambition, which in turn leads to avarice and extravagance, that Martial is reacting to in 2.91 and his several other poems on the good life. The idyllic, rural existence or lifestyle, with which he regularly counters the urban way of life, is thus in reaction to the immoderate ambition (and its ill effects) that is so typical of the city setting. Martial's intent, then, with this urban-rural contrast seems to be to lead his reader to a proper balance between natural abilities and personal aspirations, and familial and societal expectations that fuelled ambition. This premise is explored in more detail in the two sections below.

The pastoral ideal: epigram 10.47

Behind the obligations and business of the city are the national tradition and heavy family conditioning of the upper classes to achieve, with success normally gauged by money, power, and glory.[27] To counter this cultural pressure and conditioning – extremely powerful forces that run deep and often work invisibly – Martial tries to reconnect his reader with primeval nature that is equally powerful and deep-seated in its force. To do this he uses a conception of life in a rural setting, termed a pastoral ideal, almost always in antithesis to city life (as detailed in the section above). This pastoral ideal is a recurring theme in literature: it is a form of cultural primitivism that presents a return to nature as a solution to the ills that are a part of civilized society.[28] As revealed thus far, Martial's own conception of the ideal existence includes: an independence that comes from the abundance of food and supplies; simple, natural, and modest accommodations; leisure – that is, a freedom from burdensome social obligations; and a moral, healthy, and stress-free environment.[29] In epigram 10.47 Martial fills out this picture with his most complete and mature expression of his pastoral ideal:

Vitam quae faciant beatiorum,
iucundissime Martialis, haec sunt:
res non parta labore, sed relicta;
non ingratus ager, focus perennis;
lis numquam, toga rara, mens quieta;
vires ingenuae, salubre corpus;
prudens simplicitas, pares amici;
convictus facilis, sine arte mensa;
nox non ebria, sed soluta curis;
non tristis torus et tamen pudicus;
somnus qui faciat breves tenebras:
quod sis esse velis nihilque malis;
summum nec metuas diem nec optes.

10.47

Most delightful Martialis, the elements of a happier life are as
follows: money not acquired by labour, but inherited;[30] land not
unproductive; a fire year round; never a lawsuit, a toga rarely
worn, a mind at peace; a gentleman's strength, a healthy body; a
wise guilelessness, equal friends, easy company, a table without
frills; a night not drunken but free of cares; a marriage bed not
austere and yet virtuous; sleep that makes the darkness short;
wish to be what you are, wish nothing better; don't fear your last
day, nor yet pray for it.

In this poem Martial, again using an urban-rural antithesis, lists the
elements of the happy or good life, a common philosophical concern –
especially Epicurean.[31] Indeed, strains of Epicurean doctrine run
through the poem, although Martial, as usual, has tailored this description of the good life specifically for his own social community.[32]
For example, he begins with what was for him and his readership the
very important matter of adequate material subsistence: he says, the
good life includes 'money not acquired by labour, but inherited; land
not unproductive; a fire year round' (3-4). The first item – 'money not
acquired by labour, but inherited' – seems to imply that Martial means
easy money instead of that earned by working for a living. This is not,
however, an instance of laziness; rather, he is saying that a given level
of wealth – as acquired most often from a family inheritance, but also
from inheritances from friends – is necessary for that happy life, or
else one will be too invested in getting and then keeping the money
required for the level of subsistence he prescribes.[33] Epicurean doctrine did indeed caution against actively pursuing wealth, since
wealth, it was thought, would eventually enslave the pursuer; instead
it advocated a frugal, simple, and self-sufficient lifestyle.[34] Yet Martial
is hardly suggesting that his readers become part of an Epicurean
community and live in austere simplicity. Rather, first of all, his ideal
of a comfortable level of subsistence through birth or as a gift translates for his readership to a legitimate expectation and need of a
certain level of wealth because of their birth, for they would be
restricted in what they could do to acquire money;[35] and, secondly, this
ideal addresses a desire and need for leisure time as opposed to the
endless and often meaningless obligations of business in the city.[36]
From the ideal in physical sustenance Martial moves to the ideal

emotional and mental environment: with a single line – 'never a lawsuit, a toga rarely worn, a mind at peace' (5) – he characterizes the stress typically associated with city life and presents the cure offered by the pastoral ideal. He uses *lis*, which literally means 'dispute', and could include any such, but usually refers to formal disputes – that is, a lawsuit, as his illustrative example. For representing or supporting *amici* in court was one of the regular obligations of the upper classes and, just as with lawsuits today, could be very time-consuming and stressful. As for the toga, it was formal wear – of white wool, expensive in itself and also difficult both to put on and to keep clean, heavy, and thus hot in warm weather; it was worn at formal occasions, such as in the law courts, in the theatre, at the circus, and at the morning salutation – probably what Martial most had in mind here since the *salutatio* was especially irksome to him (i.e. to his poet-persona).[37] As a remedy to this urban stress and labour Martial offers a *mens quieta*, 'a mind at peace', with its association of a rural life free from the disputes and duties typical of the city – an association very common in Martial and other authors, as exampled by Martial's own context here for the phrase (coming right after complaints about lawsuits and having to wear the toga).[38]

Is, then, Martial suggesting with this line, 'never a lawsuit, a toga rarely worn, a mind at peace' (5), that his readers must, in Epicurean fashion, withdraw from public life – that is, live unnoticed (λάθε βίωσας) – in order that they may better achieve freedom and tranquility?[39] Martial, who himself (via his poet-persona) several times boasts of his own worldwide notoriety as a poet, is not likely to have been prescribing a withdrawal from public life as the ideal for his readership, most of whom would have been very active socially and politically.[40] Rather, he proposes here with this pastoral ideal of peace and tranquillity typical of a rural setting (idealistically, that is) a corrective balance to the demanding and stressful lifestyle typical for his reader.[41]

Martial next turns to the ideal physical condition for the happy or good life. *Vires ingenuae* is regularly and rightly taken to mean strength enough for one who is freeborn and of high status, but not the sort of strength required for hard, manual labour, such as that required of the lower classes.[42] Yet, *ingenuus'* primary sense of 'native', 'natural', and 'innate' suggests the naturalness of the rural environment, an environment which in contrast to the city's was regularly depicted in ancient Greek and Roman literature as healthier because of the better sun and air (thought to dispel disease) and because the physical labour required there toughened up the body.[43] Likewise for *salubre corpus*, 'a healthy body', a common desideratum, Epicurean and otherwise, but regularly associated with rural life, particularly for the upper class Romans, who saw their roots as agricultural.[44] Thus, again, beneath Martial's ideal lies an urban-rural contrast, with the city standing for the oppressive and unhealthy business environment and the country for the natural capabilities and inclinations.

The next three items or conditions Martial lists as part of the happy or good life in epigram 10.47 – 'a wise guilelessness, like friends; easy company' (7-8) – have to do with character and interpersonal relations or friendship, subjects most important to him and his readership. In his first item, *prudens simplicitas*, Martial uses *simplicitas* with its moral connotation to mean 'guilelessness' or 'innocence' that he here tempers with *prudens*, thus making it a wise or experienced innocence as opposed to a simple naiveté, the stereotype for a rustic.[45] This moralistic sense of *simplicitas* suits the context well, for, as noted with his urban-rural antithesis, Martial makes morality a necessary component of his ideal existence: specifically, the country-born *bonus vir*, 'good man', who is both honest and honourable, is played against the duplicitous, immoral, and greed-driven person stereotypical of the city.[46]

The second item of this grouping of items that have to do with character and interpersonal relations or friendship is *pares amici*, literally, 'equal' or 'like friends': this can mean either friends of the same or similar social rank, or friends alike in the sense of being well matched or congenial, with some overlap in these two senses.[47] Martial probably means friends who are well matched: that is, alike in their interests and ways of thinking, so that status and wealth are not considerations when choosing friends. For in many poems Martial castigates those who because of their high rank create distinctions in their associations – for example, by serving a lesser quality food and wine to guests lower in status.[48] In other poems he predicates what appears to be genuine friendship with those who are above him in social status on things they have in common – for example, an interest in literature and writing.[49] Julius Martialis, the addressee of epigram 10.47 and Martial's dearest friend, to judge from the epigrams, is an excellent example of what he means by equal or like friends:[50] although his senior in age, rank, and wealth, Julius is addressed in every book except two, always respectfully, often tenderly, but never obsequiously; they share an interest in literature – Julius edits Martial's poems – as well as a regard for a high quality of life. In short, Martial's ideal friendship is predicated on genuine feeling and common interests and views, and thus does not see other distinctions such as status and financial worth. The pastoral aspect of such 'equal friends' is that distinctions of rank have less significance or meaning in the country, because merit is there based more on good character, natural ability, and common cause than on a competitive and sometimes manipulative practice of either making or using so-called friends for selfishly ambitious reasons, as is characteristic of the city.

Martial's third item in this grouping of items that have to do with character and interpersonal relations or friendship is 'easy company', which means a relaxed and comfortable social intercourse in any setting, but also suggests one of the most popular social settings for the upper classes – namely, the dinner party: this is implied by the term *convictus*' secondary sense of 'entertainment' or 'feast'.[51] The dinner party was a regular topic in ancient poetry, usually as depicted through a dinner invitation – where the poet in his invitation to his addressee describes the type of dinner he intends for his potential guest.[52] Indeed, Martial's next poem of this book (10.48) is one of these dinner invitation poems, and in it he gives some definition to what he very probably means by 'easy company'. After describing in some detail the proposed menu for the dinner, Martial then says to his intended guests:

> accedent sine felle ioci nec mane timenda
>   libertas et nil quod tacuisse velis:
> de prasino conviva meus Scorpoque loquatur,
>   nec faciant quemquam pocula nostra reum.

10.48.21-4

Let there be added jokes without malice and free speaking that need not be feared in the morning, nothing you would wish you had kept silent about. Let my guest talk of the Green faction and Scorpus; let my cups make no one into a defendant.

Easy company, then, seems to consist of playful, but non-malicious talk – that is, the sort that is interesting and entertaining, but not degrading or harmful. Also, easy company seems to be characterized by being able to say what you think and feel – a tendency especially brought about by drinking ('let my cups ...') – without the fear that it will be used against you afterwards.[53] Moreover, those conversing will avoid volatile or potentially sensitive issues, as well as business concerns; rather, they will talk of the chariot races (the Green faction and Scorpus), or other light topics.[54]

The pastoral aspect of 'easy company', as with 'equal friends', shows in the inherent contrast to the nature of social intercourse in the city, particularly at a dinner party. For the typical Roman social gathering, as exemplified by the dinner party, was usually not convivial: rather, the varied ranks, character, and status of those present, along with the obligations and pressures of fulfilling duties, conferring favours, and showing respect must have made the atmosphere constrained and stressful.[55] For example, one might be seated next to someone with strong political affiliations – or even an informant (as suggested in epigram 10.48), or next to someone uncongenial by temperament or by design (e.g. a bore or a snob), or someone just unknown (cf. epigram 11.35, where all the guests at a dinner party are strangers to the poet-persona).[56] In the country, however, typically the relaxed social stratification and remoteness of political and business concerns, the unpretentious setting, and also the seemingly innate good will of the inhabitants made easy company the standard.[57]

Martial's next three items on his list of conditions of the happy or good life, 'a table without frills; a night not drunken but free of cares; a marriage bed not austere and yet virtuous' (8-10), have to do with the ideal measure in the physical appetites of food, drink, and sex. 'A table without frills' – literally, 'a table without craft' – could suggest, as does Martial's previous item (easy company), a dinner party set-ting.[58] Whether meant specifically for a dinner party or just in general, it connotes a table that is simply but amply provided, as well as a table free of ostentation, and thus recalls the pastoral ideal, with its stand-ard of naturally supplied – that is, from one's own land – and abundant provision.[59] In contrast, Martial elsewhere regularly depicts the urban table as: lavishly provided for the purpose of inducing the guest to leave the host money in his will (12.48.4); or so lavish that it makes the guests subject to gout, vomiting, and paleness (9.92.9-11; 12.48.8-10); or so indulgently ostentatious that it is pure *luxuria* – extravagance (3.22, 5.70, 10.31).

Martial's next item in this list of things relating to physical appetite is 'a night not drunken but free of cares', again with a dinner party setting possible. In other poems Martial condemns drinking to excess strongly: he depicts it variously as causing vomiting, hypocrisy and lying, shame, foolish behaviour, blindness, serious injury, and even death.[60] Not that Martial regards drinking itself as bad, for as the 'free of cares' part of his condition here in epigram 10.47 makes clear, drinking moderately could help one either to forget cares or to put aside everyday concerns in order to enjoy the moment better: in other poems he illustrates these positive effects of drinking.[61] It seems, then, that the ideal he speaks of here is a relaxed and confident or assured state brought about by the liberating quality of wine consumed in moderate amount.[62] Specifically, it frees one from the excessive stress of obligations and the pressures of business – conditions which are characteristic of the city and thus explain why the setting for his poems on excessive drinking is the city (when the setting is at all discernable, that is).

Martial's third item in his list of ideal conditions having to do with the physical appetites is 'a marriage bed not austere and yet virtuous'. As with eating and drinking habits, the previous two items on the list, Martial uses sexual behaviour to reveal character and ethics; and, as with eating and drinking, Martial recommends the mean as the ideal for sexual behaviour. Ideally, sexual practice, which Martial signifies in the poem by *torus*, 'couch' or 'bed' – usually taken to mean 'marriage bed', but not necessarily so – should be not austere or prudish (*non tristis*), but yet virtuous (*pudicus*).[63] How does this relate to a pastoral setting? *Pudicitia*, 'virtue' or 'sexual fidelity', certainly had associations with country life, as its obverse, adultery and wantonness, was more typical of the urban setting.[64] At the same time, the liberal sexual attitude implied by 'not austere', although it can appear contradictory to the stereotype of the virtuous and faithful country boy or girl, is actually closer to a natural – that is, nature-based – mentality or outlook:[65] for example, the person living in the country will probably witness animals breeding and be less inhibited about these instinctual drives and their expression; also there will be a forthrightness about bodily functions. The city-dweller, on the other hand, will be hedged in by an artificial and sanitized environment, as well as by restrictions and sanctions made necessary by class distinctions and by the close and potentially dangerous conditions – both physical (dense population) and emotional (high degree of stress).

Martial's next item or ingredient for the happy or good life, 'sleep that makes the darkness short' (11) is an elaboration on 'a mind at peace' from line 5 of the poem – an item which Martial counterposed to the stress and contentiousness typical of the urban setting. Here the phrasing either suggests a night that is untroubled by anxiety that causes sleeplessness – once again a feature of Epicureanism;[66] or it implies simply being able to sleep through the night uninterrupted by noise or by very early social, business, and political obligations – both interpretations with an inherent contrast to sleeping conditions in the city. That is, the contrast to the Epicurean sense of untroubled sleep would be the difficulty in getting sleep because of the stress and pressures of business, political, and property matters normally centred in the city.[67] As for the sense of simply being able to sleep the night through uninterrupted, which is the likelier interpretation, Martial undoubtedly has in mind two types of interruptions, both typical of the city. The first would be the noise of commercial traffic: illustrations of this come at epigram 9.68, where the poet is forced to lie awake the entire night because of an overly noisy schoolmaster who keeps his pupils very late; and at epigram 12.57, where the noise of the various professions of the city – moneychangers, coppersmiths, beggars, and pedlars – prevent sleep. The second type of interruption would occur because of the early morning salutation – something Martial complains of repeatedly. For example, at epigram 1.49 he says that when you live in the country, nowhere will you see the clothing of a patrician, and far away will be court attendants and the grumbling client, and imperious widows, and 'no pale defendant will interrupt your deep slumber; instead you will sleep all morning' (1.49.31-6). Similarly, at epigram 12.18, in address to Juvenal, Martial contrasts his life in the country to Juvenal's life in the city. He says specifically of his own sleeping habits: 'I enjoy an enormous and indecent amount of sleep, which often not even the third hour interrupts, and I repay myself now in full for my thirty-year-long vigil' (12.18.13-16).[68] As these various examples suggest, the country is more conducive to sleep because it is quieter, without commercial traffic, and free of social, business, and political obligations.[69]

Martial's last two conditions at epigram 10.47 of the happy or good life, 'wish to be what you are, wish nothing better; don't fear your last day, nor yet pray for it' (12-13), are actually states of mind or consciousness that would indicate the realization of the good life. That is, with the previous fifteen items or conditions listed in the poem Martial has tried to recall for his readers their natural and primeval nature by means of a pastoral ideal, always presented against the implied adverse conditions of the city – the city which represents the great pressures on the upper classes to achieve and succeed. With these two final injunctions Martial tests his readers, so to speak, on their condition or state: for, to the degree that they have attained these states of consciousness (wish to be what you are ...; don't fear your last day ...), then to that degree they have balanced their heavy national and familial conditioning with their individualistic abilities and aspirations. More specifically, this so-called test works as follows: with the first injunction, 'wish to be what you are, wish nothing better', Martial in effect says to his readers, 'You must be satisfied with what you are and not be envious of or begrudge others their lot. For, if you are dissatisfied with what you are and want something more, then you have become overzealous in your drive to achieve, and are in fact greedy and selfishly acquisitive.'[70] Then, with the second injunction, 'don't fear your last day, nor yet pray for it', Martial effectively tells his readers: 'Fearing death indicates that you're not content with your life because you can't let go of it when it's time; this, in turn, shows your grasping and greedy nature – how you just can't be satisfied. As for wanting to die, this shows you as both cowardly and dissatisfied because you can't accept and endure what you are.'[71]

In sum, with these two last injunctions Martial has recalled his attack on avarice and excessive ambition, behind which are the upper classes' heavy societal and familial conditioning to achieve. He has represented this conditioning in the poem with the implied contrast of the dehumanizing obligations and conditions of the city. To counter this cultural pressure and conditioning Martial has used a pastoral ideal, as embodied in the fifteen items or conditions of the happy life, to reconnect his readers with their personal abilities and aspirations. The effect throughout has been to bring his readers to a proper balance between societal expectations, on the one hand, and personal wants and needs, on the other. Then, with the last two injunctions of the poem, he tests his readers' success at attaining that balance between personal and societal needs.

The golden age of Saturn

The pastoral ideal that Martial uses at epigram 10.47 and in other poems to represent the good life has further significance: its typical components – sustenance in abundance attained with little labour, which, in turn, allows for much leisure time, and also an innocence and easy concord among humans – connect it with the mythical time of the golden age, a familiar motif in ancient Greek and Roman literature. As Leach puts it:

> Behind the pastoral vision lies the archetype of the primeval paradise, commonly called the golden age or the garden of Eden, and from these associations the pastoral draws its ideal coloring.[72]

This connection between Martial's pastoral ideal and a golden age gives his conception of the good life more strength – something it needs in order to counteract the powerful national and familial conditioning of the upper classes to achieve. Also the pastoral ideal's connection to the concept of the golden age reveals more of the meaning and effect of Martial's poetry.

First, some definition of the golden age. The initial description comes from Hesiod: as he describes it, when Cronus ruled, mortals lived like gods, free from sorrow, labour, and grief; they spent their time happily feasting, beyond the reach of all evils, living in ease and peace on their lands, plentifully supplied, and beloved of the gods; this age ended with Zeus taking power and sending Cronus to rule over the Islands of the Blest; afterwards, succeeding ages of humanity only declined in quality.[73] This description is prototypical in its components: physical sustenance naturally supplied; the absence of all negative or base emotions; an innocent, blessed, or happy state, but of limited term and followed by worse conditions.

The Roman version of the golden age is, as might be expected, somewhat different, although it keeps the prototypical components of the Greek golden age.[74] In the Roman literary tradition Saturn (Saturnus), who was very probably an archaic Roman agricultural deity, is merged or identified with Cronus.[75] In Vergil's account of this golden age – coming primarily from the *Aeneid* – Saturn keeps his original identity as a Roman agricultural divinity: after he is driven from Olympus by his son, Jupiter, he seeks refuge in Italy, is made king there, and through his civilizing influence upon the savage inhabitants – through the introduction of agriculture, as revealed in other sources – brings a golden age of peace to the natives; gradually, however, this golden age gives way to the 'love of possession' (*amor habendi*), or avarice, in other words, as well as to the 'madness of warfare' (*belli rabies*).[76] Macrobius' account is similar in the main, but differs in some details: Saturn arrives as an exile in Italy when Janus is ruler there and is taught agriculture by the exiled god.[77] The standard of life is thereby improved, for before Saturn came humans were brutish and crude. In gratitude Janus makes Saturn his co-ruler. Macrobius adds that Saturn was credited with inventing the art of grafting, the cultivation of fruit trees, the discovery of honey, and the instructing of humans in the fertilization of fields; his reign was said to be a time of great happiness because of the abundance of sustenance and because there was no slavery.

In what may be termed the Roman literary version of the golden age myth, Saturn's golden age reign is depicted as occurring while he was the ruler of the heavens, just as in Hesiod's account. Ovid's account in the *Metamorphoses* is typical of this version: as he tells it, during Saturn's reign there was no need of judges or laws because deception and crime were unknown; there was no war; the earth provided all sustenance in abundance with no labour required; and the environment and climate were ideal (1.89-112). In a similar account of Saturn's reign from his *Amores* Ovid adds in a strong moral component – namely, how, in contrast to his own age, the golden age was free of avarice; this moral component was typical of the Roman treatment of the myth (Martial's included). Ovid phrases it thus: when Saturn ruled heaven 'the deep earth kept all lucre in darkness and hid away bronze, silver, gold, and heavy iron from all hands' (3.8.36-8). Instead, the earth provided, as Ovid tells it, grains, fruits, and honey without any labour required; there was no marking off of land, and no one sailed on the seas. Ovid then berates humankind for being too skilful and clever to its ruin; what benefit did it get from warfare, he asks, or from sailing the seas (3.8.39-52). Finally, he ends the passage with this condemnation of his own age:

> We dig up from the earth solid gold instead of grains. The soldier possesses wealth gotten with blood. The senate house shuts out the poor: a person's material worth gives him public office. Thence comes the grave judge; Thence comes the stern equestrian.
>
> Ov. Am. 3.8.53-6

Presaging Martial's treatment of the topic, Ovid describes his own age as preoccupied with the aggressive, even bloody, acquisition of wealth – wealth which can buy one honours and glory in the form of public office. This ethical or moral element, which is only implied in Hesiod's version, is typically accentuated in the Roman accounts.

Martial, in his only direct account of Saturn's reign, follows in the same ethical vein, as exemplified above by Ovid. In his account Martial invokes Saturn for the yearly feast given in his honour at his holiday, the Saturnalia, by Martial's friend, Priscus:

> Antiqui rex magne poli mundique prioris
>   sub quo pigra quies nec labor ullus erat,
> nec regale nimis fulmen nec fulmine digni,
>   scissa nec ad Manes, sed sibi dives humus:
> laetus ad haec facilisque veni sollemnia Prisci
>   gaudia: cum sacris te decet esse tuis.
>
> 12.62.1-6

> Great king of ancient heaven and a former world, under whom was a lazy repose, not any labour, nor too regal a thunderbolt, nor any deserving of a thunderbolt, nor was the ground cut to the spirit world, but its riches were kept to itself: come happy and obliging to these yearly festivities of Priscus. It's fitting that you be with your rites.

Martial's conception of Saturn's golden age includes the traditional labour-free existence; also that the era was punishment-free because there was no crime – as Martial puts it, none were deserving of the thunderbolt.[78] Martial, like Ovid, also adds in the moralistic contrast to his own time's avarice: back during Saturn's reign there was no mining of precious metals that brings people wealth. Finally, by invoking Saturn for his festive rites Martial illustrates the connection between the festival of the Saturnalia and the reign of Saturn: for the Romans saw the Saturnalia as a brief return to the age of Saturn with its ideal conditions.[79]

A description of the Saturnalia may be helpful here.[80] The festival began on 17 December with a sacrifice (*sacrificium publicum*) and then a public meal (*convivium publicum*) before the temple of Saturn; shops, the law-courts, and schools were closed; the holiday, although initially confined to one day, during the late Republic and Empire lasted anywhere from three to five to seven days. Private celebrations – the beginning of which were marked by the cry *Io Saturnalia* – began after the public banquet; these celebrations were characterized by their licence and reversal of behaviour. For example, the toga was exchanged for the informal *synthesis*, an outfit of matching undergarment and mantle; soft caps (*pilei*), which symbolized freedom (e.g. given to freed slaves), were worn by the normally bare-headed populace; gambling, normally illegal, was permitted, as was heavy drinking (also usually punishable) and banqueting; slaves dined with their masters and were permitted to speak freely to them; gifts of various types, some of a formalized type (e.g. wax or clay figurines), were exchanged; and at private banquets satire and derision, replete with obscenity and sexual content, were the practice.[81]

The effect of this licence and reversal of normal behaviour during the Saturnalia can reveal more about Martial's conception of the good life. Versnel, in his investigation of ancient Greek and Roman festivals of reversal, describes what has been the orthodox explanation: reversal rituals have been thought to provide a safety-valve in their release of pent up aggression in a controlled setting.[82] Versnel adds to this orthodox explanation another closely related one – what he calls 'the function of legitimation or confirmation of the social *status quo*': through the contrast of the chaos typical of reversal, such rituals make people aware of the rightness of the normal social order and thus give cohesion to that order.[83] Then, as a further development of the social cohesion theory, Versnel gives his own theory: he posits that reversal rituals give a 'deep legitimacy' to the particular institutional order a society imposes on reality when that construct is challenged.[84] Such 'deep legitimacy' can come only through a return to a mythical reality that is outside that society – beyond its borders of history and space; this 'other reality' embodies an eternal truth that existed before time but still exists behind it and behind present reality, and occasionally is mingled with it during 'periods of exception' – that is, during naturally occurring periods of crisis (e.g. at the assassination of a king or president) or during ceremonially created reversal rituals (such as the Saturnalia).[85]

Versnel's theory of the effect of Saturnalian reversal rituals – that they give deep legitimacy to a society through contact with an 'other reality' – also applies to Martial's representation of the good life through a pastoral ideal. For both the Saturnalia and a pastoral ideal call up a mythical reality – namely, the golden age of Saturn, with its ideal conditions. The purpose of the holiday, as with the purpose of Martial's representation of the good life via a pastoral ideal, was to reacquaint participants with the primeval reality behind their socially constructed world.[86] For example, the feasting of the holiday as well as the gift-giving recalls the time when the abundant and readily available resources were shared equally by all – the other reality. This is a reminder to persons that the yet abundant natural resources could and should be shared equitably instead of being amassed by a select few to the detriment of many others – this amassing of resources being the social construct wherein the upper classes were strongly conditioned to achieve through acquisition.[87] Not that the festival of the Saturnalia or Martial with his Saturnalian verse is prescribing a return to a primeval state of communal property: rather, both the holiday ritual and Martial are encouraging that ambition be moderated, or else the avarice and extravangance occasioned by excessive ambition will destroy the system of social exchange whereby resources are shared.

On a more personal level, both the Saturnalia with its reversal rituals and Martial with his pastoral ideal have the effect of freeing people from the restrictive and sometimes oppressive social constraints long enough for them to realize their personal capabilities and aspirations.[88] As Leach expresses it in speaking of Vergil's pastoral ideal in his *Eclogues*:

4. The Good Life

The desire to enter the pastoral world – to recreate in imagination the infancy of mankind – is the expression of a longing for rebirth, for the awakening of some freer, hitherto unrealized self whose potential has been repressed by the limitations of mortal nature or everyday life.[89]

For Martial this means that he acquainted his readers with a reality that was both primitivistic and utopian in order to make them aware of any wrongness or inappropriateness or imbalance of the social construct they were living. For that social construct had been imposed on them by familial and national conditioning so ingrained and pervasive that it would have remained invisible except for the stark contrast of the Saturnalian rituals and Martial's expression of a pastoral ideal.

In sum, this primitivistic world view which Martial used in his poems to represent the good life is meant to address the seemingly inevitable ills that attend a complex and civilized society – specifically, the sometimes mindless and despiritualizing conditioning and constraints that society imposes on the individual, and also the excessive labour it necessitates in order to attain what is considered adequate for a civilized existence. Martial, in opposition to an artificial and degrading existence that he reckons as a waste of life, counterposes a vision of a golden age existence: a return to humankind's primeval and communal state during the reign of Saturn.

Conclusion

My Rome praises, loves and recites my books; and every pocket,
every hand holds me. Look, a certain person turns red, becomes
pale, is stunned, gapes, hates. This I want: now my poems
please me.

Martial 6.60

Martial's impact on today's reader of his poetry varies dramatically:
some think his poetry trivial and a waste of time, or even see it as
objectionable because of its obscenity and sexual content; most see it
purely as entertainment; and some believe it has significance and even
a serious message. Martial's own intent, as expressed through the
poems, is ambiguous if not contradictory: most of the time he acknow-
ledges that his poetry is for entertainment, but then, though not often,
he claims, or at least implies, more purpose and significance to it. In
order to get at any purpose or significance beyond entertainment this
study has viewed Martial's twelve-book collection in the context of the
Indo-European tradition of blame and praise poetry – in particular, in
the tradition of the ancient Greek iambic poets. Poets who worked in
this tradition, even though they employed a personal and confidential
style and tone, addressed communal interests as related to individual
concerns. In other words, they addressed issues important to the
functioning and success of their social group, even though they ap-
proached them from a personal or individualistic vantage point. As
part of this tradition, wherein they always represented the interests
of the social community, they were granted special licence in their
writing – specifically, subject-matter, language, and candour much beyond normal social limits. As a result, their writing had great power to
influence because it spoke directly, forthrightly, and with visceral images
that bypassed social and cultural filters to reach the emotions directly.

Following in this tradition, Martial with his epigram, itself a per-
mutation of Roman *vers de société* – social verse, *à la* Catullus in

particular – represented the feelings and interests of his social group, for the most part the upper classes of the early Empire. To suit his political environment and his message, he gave his poetry a festive and playful spirit – he sometimes characterized it as Saturnalian verse; but yet, like the Saturnalian rituals, it had an underlying sense and effect that contributed to the health and success of his social community. For Martial's reversals of tradition in his verse – his taboo language and subject-matter, his socially shocking frankness, his delight in the primeval and natural functions that define and unite all humankind, and his intolerance for the socially and artificially constructed boundaries such as status and wealth – all acknowledge and validate basic human needs, while doing so in a way that is mindful and supportive of societal needs and constraints.

Besides considering the place of Martial's twelve-book collection in the literary tradition, this study has looked at the social and cultural views that are the background or setting for Martial's verse – views that usually go unexplained in the poems because they are assumed as understood by the reader. Yet, one must know this social and cultural context to understand the direction and effect of the poems. For example, one must realize that for the ancient Romans gift-giving was the beginning and proof of friendship in order to realize that Martial's frequent treatment of reciprocity was not at all an obsession with material wealth. Rather, Martial's repeated handling of reciprocity indicated a strong concern for a healthy community, which had its basis in the good faith established by the equitable give and take of interpersonal relationships. For the Roman community – the Roman Empire – was built around just such a concept of social community: it was one of the keys to their great success and power. However, this concept of reciprocity as key to interpersonal as well as international relationships is a very hard lesson for many readers. Our cultural filters make us sceptical and blind: we tend to view a conscious gift-exchange as manipulation – an attempt to buy good faith or loyalty – instead of as the building block of relationships and community.

Similarly, for the modern day reader Martial's philosophy of life, as considered in the previous chapter, is hardly weighty or original – at least on the face of it. Yet, in its cultural context his concept of the good life was stunning and highly provocative – much like advising present day college graduates in business that making money and acquiring a prestigious position are not all important to their lives and happiness. Although this guidance may not be profound, it certainly is important on an emotional, and perhaps even a spiritual, level: it functions as a meaningful check on societal pressures that are likely to go completely unexamined and unchecked otherwise. Present day readers can understand and benefit from this message. For, just as those of the ancient Roman upper classes who were driven unknowingly by national tradition and familial conditioning to achieve were careless of the dangers to person and especially to social community of the selfish amassing of wealth, so today are we, who are relentlessly conditioned and driven to make and spend money without limit, generally blind to the harm in it, both to ourselves and especially to our community at large.

In short, an informed reading of Martial's poetry, which requires an understanding of the literary tradition and social context, is a lesson in what makes a healthy and successful individual who can best contribute to the social community. For, working in the iambic tradition, Martial treats his readership as a psychologist or counsellor would treat an individual. In large part Martial does this via his invective with his candid representation of the basest and most humanistic instincts and feelings in opposition to the crushing weight of conditioning and social strictures. Sometimes he shocks the socially unbalanced reader back into awareness with the degree of his candidness and his obscenity. This has the effect of putting his readers in better touch with their humanity, and thus makes them better aware of and more comfortable with themselves and their place in the social community.

Notes

Introduction

1. Sullivan 1987, 178; cf. also Sullivan 1991, 115, with n. 1, where he presents the same summation in a slightly expanded form.

2. Cf. also Otto Seel's appraisal of Martial ('Ansatz zu einer Martial-Interpretation', *A&A* 10 [1961]: 53-76 = G. Pfohl (ed.), *Das Epigramm. Zur Geschichte einer inschriftlichen und literarischen Gattung* [Darmstadt 1969], 153-86) which is, as noted by Grewing (ed.) 1998, 7-10, a summarization of the nineteenth- and twentieth-century view of Martial as a mediocre poet whose works were the result of a morally depraved mind. Also cf. Sullivan 1993, for a chronologically arranged survey of criticism of Martial's poetry from Martial's own day down through most of the twentieth century, including an abbreviated version of Seel's article (180-202) in English translation.

3. Cf., e.g., the substantially different treatment Holzberg gives to Martial's poetry in his two separate books on him (Holzberg 1988 and 2002) – see the helpful review of the latter by F. Grewing in *BMCR* 2003.07.20 (http://ccat.sas.upenn.edu/bmcr/2003/2003-07-20.html), which highlights the dramatic differences in the irreconcilable interpretations Holzberg gives to Martial's poetry.

4. Ker 1919, xv.

5. Ker 1919, xvi, n. 3. This unexplained choice of Italian for these 'wholly impossible ones' prompted the versatile translator, Rolfe Humphries, to comment that it was done 'on the theory that God doesn't understand Italian' (this anecdote comes from K.J. Reckford, 'Shameless Interests: The Decent Scholarship of Indecency', *American Journal of Philology* 117 [1996]: 311). Ker used the Italian translations of Giuspanio Graglia, which were originally published in the late 1700s.

6. Cf., e.g., studies such as M. Foucault, *History of Sexuality, Vol. I: An Introduction* (New York 1978), where the historical constructs of sexuality are perceived as encoded strategies of knowledge and power. A good example of such a study on Martial and the Roman satirists is Richlin 1992.

7. E.g. at epigram 1.35.14-15 Martial says that to take the obscenity from his poems is like castrating Priapus, a fertility god – see further at Ch. 2.

8. E.T. Salmon, *A History of the Roman World from 30 BC to AD 138* (London 1959) 266.

9. J. Bramble from 'Martial and Juvenal', ch. 29 of E.J. Kenney (ed.),

Cambridge History of Classical Literature II, Latin Literature (Cambridge 1982), 600.

10. In defining his literary programme Martial uses the persona of the poet: this poet-persona is the author of the collection, and appears again and again throughout the twelve books in a variety of settings and contexts. I have taken care to make the distinction between Martial himself and his poet-persona: I use the term 'poet-persona', or just 'poet', in regard to information presented within the poems, even if some of the information is verified by outside sources as true of Martial himself (e.g. his birthplace being Bilbilis); and I make Martial himself responsible for the writing and structuring of the book collection. I apologize for any awkwardness that has resulted.

11. Cf. e.g. R.G. Turner, 'Levels of Intent in Martial', in *ANRW* 2.32.4 (1986): 2626-77; also cf. the concept of a subversive subtext to Martial's imperial panegyric, on which see Ch. 3.

12. On determining authorial intentions see Heath 2002, 59-97 (as cited and discussed by Grewing 2003, 1056), wherein Heath first addresses the main misconceptions about 'intentionism' – i.e. the conception of 'the author as an agent, and of the text as the product of an agent's purposive behaviour' (60); and then in the rest of the chapter (79-97) defends the premise that these intentions are knowable. Heath concludes that authorial intentions '... can be known *up to a point*, but not *ultimately*' (p. 82).

13. Sullivan 1991, 115.

14. See Boyle 1995b, 252ff., on the 'revolutionary' nature of Sullivan's monograph on Martial; Boyle notes that Sullivan's achievement was best reflected 'not in the eulogistic reviews of peers but in the letters he received after the publication of the book from fledgling Ph.D. students, deterred by their advisors from pursuing work on Martial the trivial poetaster or 'court jester' (to use Bramble's dismissive term), who now felt emboldened to devote the crucial dissertation years to the Flavian poet' (252).

15. Shackleton Bailey 1993.

16. Grewing (ed.) 1998 for the essay collection; also see Iso Echegoyen and Encuentra Ortega 2004, for a collection of papers on various aspects of Martial's poetry that has recently appeared; Citroni 1975 and Howell 1980 on Book 1; Kay 1985 on Book 11; Howell 1995 on Book 5; Leary 1996 on Book 14; Grewing 1997 on Book 6; Henriksén 1998/99 on Book 9; Leary 2001 on Book 13; Galán Vioque 2002 on Book 7; Schöffel 2002 on Book 8; cf. Watson and Watson 2003 on selections; Williams 2004 on Book 2; Damschen and Heil 2004 on Book 10.

17. Book-length studies: Holzberg 2002; Lorenz 2002; Scherf 2001; Obermayer 1998.

18. This study has been limited to Martial's twelve-book collection; thus far only a limited amount of work has been done on the other three books that comprise Martial's total output – e.g. see Leary 1996 and 2001 on Books 13 and 14.

19. See Ward 1973, on the Indo-European poet-singer tradition, and see

128-9 for Archilochus' invective as part of it; Ward uses as evidence the similarity of metrical structures employed by the poets of the various traditions (Greek, Celtic, Germanic, and Vedic), as well as similarity in content, purpose, and significance of the poetry.

20. Ward 1973, 127. Elliott 1960, 15-18, adds in the Arabic tradition of invective (*hijá*), where the poet's chief function was to compose verse against the tribal enemy (15).

21. See Ward 1973, 131-5, for various examples of the dire effects blame verse could have on the victim (e.g. raised warts on the face; a king blinds himself in order to avoid attack through invective song; victims driven into exile or even to suicide). Also see Elliott 1960, 3-15, 49-65 on the origins of satire in magic and ritual. Elliott's theory is that satire came from primitive spells and curses with a bipartite function: 'to invoke life-giving influences', such as fertility; and 'to expel blight and dearth and evil', which were often embodied in an individual – a scapegoat, who was driven from the community (58-9).

22. On the connections between religious ritual, Greek iambic poetry, Old Comedy, and Roman satire and epigram see Ch. 1.

23. See Gerber 1999, 1-2; also West 1974, 22-39 for a history of iambus, and especially 22 for the various metres (epodes, trimeters, trochaic tetrameters, choliambic trimeters and tetrameters, hexameters or half-hexameters) and poets (at least ten) included in the iambic tradition. Also see Ch. 2 for a detailed account of the nature of ancient Greek iambics.

24. Nagy in Cavarzere 2001, ix. Iambic idea is a transliteration of ἰαμβικὴ ἰδέα, an expression used by Aristotle *Poet.* 1448b30, where he asserts that it is the origin of comedy. See Koster 1980, 7-21; and this volume, Ch 1.

25. On invective as the outstanding feature of iambics see Ch. 1. See also Gerber 1999, 1-4.

26. First suggested by Dover 1963, 189; adopted and argued by West 1974, 23-5, who notes the associations of iambi with the rituals of Demeter and Dionysus: specifically, West compares ἴαμβος with διθύραμβος, θρίαμβος, and ἴθυμβος, all songs composed for religious, festive occasions; also cf. Rosen 1988, 4 with n. 14.

27. See Gerber 1999, 4: 'With regard to the occasion for the delivery of iambus we are again lacking secure evidence from the extant verses, but it seems safe to say that one at least of the main occasions was the symposium.'

28. Mankin 1995, 8. The concept of the audience as *philoi* and the iambus as an affirmation of *philotês* is originally from Nagy 1979, 251.

29. See Citroni, 1989, 215ff., who argues that Books 7, 11, 13, 14, probably 4 and 5, and possibly the first edition of 10 were released for the Saturnalia; Nauta 2002, 112 and 130 adds in Books 12 and 8; on the nature and significance of the festival itself, see Ch. 4.

30. E.g. 1.4.5-7; 2.1.9; 5.16.9; 7.97.11; 11.17. On the symposium and other public fora as a context for the reception of Martial's books see Nauta 2002, 139-41 and 166-80.

31. For a history of Latin epigram before Martial see especially Kay 1985,

9-13, who gives examples of the earliest epigrams; also Holzberg 2002, 24-8; Citroni 1996, 536-8; and Sullivan 1991, 93-100.

32. As Kay 1985, 10, n. 21, puts it when explaining the varied form of these earliest literary Latin epigrams: 'but epigram also seems to have had a much wider signification for the Romans than for us, including any reasonably short poem which its author did not label by another name.'

33. See Citroni 1996, 537, who dates this type of verse to Catulus (consul 102 BCE); as he puts it: 'With Catulus the epigram becomes for the first time at Rome the ideal genre for the leisure hours of the refined and recherché upper-class amateur. From the time of Cicero we have many references to (and a few fragments of) short poems written for pleasure and cultural display by leading Romans ...'.

34. On Roman *vers de société*, see Spisak 1992, 12-14. The definition for *vers de société* from *The Concise Oxford Dictionary of Literary Terms* (by C. Baldrick; Oxford, 1990) is: 'the French term ('society verse') for a kind of light verse that deals with the frivolous concerns of upper-class social life, usually in a harmlessly playful vein of satire and with technical elegance.'

35. Newman 1990, viii-ix and 72; for details see his chapter, 'The Ἰαμβικὴ Ἰδέα', 43-74. The idea that Archilochus was Catullus' single most important literary model is not new: cf., e.g. R. Ellis, *A Commentary on Catullus*, 2nd edn (Oxford 1889), xxxix; on Catullus' connection with the Indo-European tradition of blame and praise poetry (including Archilochus and Hipponax), see Wray 1996, 37-130.

36. Newman 1990, 52-9. The traditional perception of Archilochus, Hipponax, and Simonides is that they wrote primarily from personal experiences and that their main purpose was to settle scores with actual people who had offended them.

37. Dover 1963, 201-4; Dover's list is duplicated by Newman, 52-3.

38. See 2.71, 4.14, 5.5, 7.99, 10.103; and especially 10.78.14-16.

39. For the many similarities between Martial and Catullus see Swann 1994, 3-9; Watson and Watson 2003, 35-6; G. Lee, *The Poems of Catullus* (Oxford and New York 1990), xivff. on 'Catullus the Epigrammatist'; and Mendell 1922, 3-4.

40. See Ferguson 1963 on the similarities between Martial and Catullus. Mendell 1922, 20, concludes that Catullus' contribution to the development of Latin epigram was an invective tone.

41. Sullivan 1991, 96; Sullivan goes on to note that this personal element was not as prevalent in the more formal and objective Greek epigrammatic tradition.

42. Newman 1990, 72, connects Martial, in his adoption of the Archilochean ἰαμβικὴ ἰδέα, with Catullus, and hence considers him also as part of the iambic tradition; see also 75-103, Newman's chapter 'Catullus and Martial'.

1. Invective

1. St Columba (sixth century CE) to King Aed, in W. Stokes (trans.), 'The Eulogy of Saint Columba', *Revue Celtique* 22: 45 (1899), as cited by Ward 1973, 132, as representative of the earliest Irish tradition – the Old-Irish.

2. On the tradition of blame poets see primarily Ward 1973.

3. Ward introduces the verse addressed to King Aed by saying: 'The unusual power wielded by the poets was recognized by ... St. Columba ... who felt it necessary to warn King Aed that the singers were capable of both praise and blame' (132). Then Ward notes that in 575 CE King Aed 'sought to eliminate the entire profession of the *filid*, the poet-singers' (Ward 1973, 134-5; Ward cites as his source H. Meroney, 'Studies in Early Irish Satire', *Journal of Celtic Studies* 2 [1953], 222). On the power of the Greek iambic poets, see below the story of Lycambes and his daughters, who were driven to suicide by verses of Archilochus, the Greek iambic poet. Hipponax, another Greek iambic poet, was said to have driven two sculptors to suicide with his verse because they had caricatured him with a sculpture (Plin. *HN* 36.5).

4. On the number of satiric poems in Martial's twelve-book collection cf. Szelest 1986, 2584, n. 40, who calculates the rough percentage of satiric epigrams in each of the twelve books, with a range of 33% to 75%; this averages out to about 55%.

5. See Grewing 1997, 529, on Martial's *ioci*.

6. See Brown 1997, 13-42, for a thorough account of the genre of iambos, including its possible origins in the myth of Iambe (16ff.).

7. See, e.g., the comments of Richardson 1974, 213-17; and H.P. Foley, *The Homeric Hymn to Demeter* (Princeton 1994), 45-8: as proof, both adduce humorous abuse as a part of the cult rituals of Demeter (mentioned in Apollodorus 1.5.1 and in Diodorus Siculus 5.4.7); also the fact that the Greek words in the text used for Iambe's joking are the same as used for personal abuse or invective directed at someone; and finally, that obscenity is traditionally a part of iambic poetry. Brown 1997, 21-4, considers later *testimonia* on Iambe and her dealings with Demeter and arrives at the same conclusion – i.e. that Iambe's comments to Demeter took the form of abuse, using words not normally permitted (24).

8. On this and other versions of the Baubo myth, see Olender 1990, 87ff.

9. Clement *Protreptikos* 2.20.1 = Orph. fr. 52 (Kern).

10. See Olender 1990, 94-7, on this passage and the connection in ritual between obscenity and fertility.

11. See Arthur 1994, 229, with n. 26 for further references: Arthur refers to the Baubo figurines from Priene in Asia Minor.

12. On laughter Richardson 1974, 217, says: 'Laughter is often a symbol of rebirth, or of restoration of the dead to life'; also see Arthur 1994, 229. For the healing and socializing effects of laughter, as well as its associations with fertility, see Segal 2001, 23-6.

13. Brown 1997, 41. On inversion and its effect see further Ch. 4 on the Saturnalia.

14. Ritual abuse was directly associated with the cults of Demeter and Dionysus through various festivals such as the Haloa, the Stenia, the Thesmophoria, and the initiation rites of the Eleusinian Mysteries – see Miller 1994, 25; Miralles and Pòrtulas 1983, 22-4, 112-16; Reckford 1987, 464-7; Rosen 1988, 4; Richardson 1974, 213-17.

15. See Brown 1997, 25-36, who, after surveying the evidence for cult-song used at ritual occasions, concludes: ἴαμβος of the sort practised by Archilochus and the other Ionian iambists is clearly a "literary" crystallization of cult-song or, in other words, a poetic genre that has developed from cult-song' (36).

16. Archil. *Testt.* 5-11 (Gerber) on Archilochus' birthplace; for the cult of Demeter at Paros see Richardson 1974, 321-2, at line 491, where Paros is mentioned as one of Demeter's sites.

17. Archil. *Test.* 65 (Gerber) = Paus. 10.28.3; also see Brown 1997, 45-7, and Richardson 1974, 214.

18. Archil. *Testt.* 3, 34, and 67 (Gerber), as well as Plato *Ion* 531a (as cited by Gerber 1999, 4); see also Brown 1997, 13, and Miller 1994, 26-7.

19. The story is from Archil. *Test.* 3A, col. III (Gerber), which, as Gerber 1999, 25, n.1, says: 'seems to refer to the contents of fr. 251': 'Dionysus ... unripe grapes ... sweet(?) figs ... Oipholios', where grapes and figs may be sexual metaphors for young or small breasts and vaginas, and Oipholios is presumed 'an epithet of Dionysus and derived from the root οἰθ-, denoting sexual intercourse' – Gerber 1999, 249, on fr. 251, ns 1 and 2. For a reconstruction of the story, see Gerber 1999, 3, Brown 1997, 46-7, and West 1974, 24-5.

20. The Greek word ἰαμβικώτερο[ν, translated here as 'too iambic', could also, as Gerber 1999, 25, with n. 1, notes, be translated as 'in too iambic a manner'.

21. See Gerber 1999, 3, who uses the term 'literary iambus'; also see Henderson 1991, 17-19, who specifically says that the origins of Archilochus' iambic poetry 'are to be found in the abusive αἰσχρολογία of the cults' (18), and further maintains that Archilochus 'was personally involved in the cult songs of Paros ... and worked in part from the inspiration he received from them' (18). On the general connection between satire and religious festivals and rituals see Newman 1990, 44-5; cf. Richlin 1992, 10.

22. On the close association of iambic verse and Old Comedy see Henderson 1991, 14-19; and Rosen 1988, 4 and passim.

23. See Koster 1980, 55-62, on the Greek iambists. For a list of the primary and secondary obscenities used by the Greek iambic poets see Henderson 1991, 19-23; for obscene jokes in Old Comedy see Henderson 1991, 108-222.

24. See Gerber 1999, Archilochus *Testt.* 19-32; all sources of the story are unanimous except on the suicides – see Brown 1997, 50-69, who considers variant interpretations.

25. See Burnett 1983, 19-23, on Lycambes and his daughters as 'creatures of the poet's own fictions' (20); in her chapter on Archilochus' life (15-32) Burnett debunks the popular notion of Archilochus as 'a bastard and a mercenary, a bitter pragmatist who hated tradition and sang with the lewd voice of revolt and poverty, a drunkard who fought with both friend and enemy, a rebel against worn-out values, a debunker of aristocratic ideals, a brawling upstart with a vein of music in him' (15-16). Rather, Burnett argues: that Archilochus was treated almost as a demigod by his contemporaries (16-17); that he worked within a well-established poetic tradition (30); and that his poems and their poet-personae were largely fictions created mostly for the purpose of entertainment (30-2).

26. Brown 1997, 69. Cf. West 1974, 27, who suggests that 'Lycambes and his libidinous daughters were not living contemporaries of Archilochus but stock characters in a traditional entertainment with some (perhaps forgotten) ritual basis'; also Nagy 1979, 248-9; and Miller 1994, 28-9.

27. See Wray 1996, 47ff., on ancient invective as a 'means of non-violent control' and as serving to enforce certain social norms of behaviour; Wray cites G. Dumézil, *Servius et la Fortune: Essai sur la fonction sociale de louange et de blâme et sur les éléments indo-européens du cens romain* (Paris 1943), passim. Also cf. Burnett 1983, 60: 'The singer of defamatory song ... practised an art that was conscious and traditional, one that maintained the health of the community, and consequently it will be egregiously wrong to take the slanders of Archilochus as the mere raw outburst of an angry young man who happened to have a lyre in his hands.'

28. See especially Reckford 1987, 15: '... [o]bscenity is one way of expressing and celebrating the richness of life ...'; and his appendices on Carnival Concentration: Halloween and Anthesteria (452-560); Dionysus and the Phallus (457-60); and *Aischrologia* (461-7). The concept of carnival in Bakhtin 1984a, 110, is certainly related, although Bakhtin sees carnival more as an attack on social norms and institutions, whereas the iambic poet uses the carnival licence to attack threats to social norms and institutions – see further Nauta 2002, 183-4; and this volume Ch. 4, on the section on the Saturnalia.

29. For a survey treatment of invective in ancient Roman literature see Koster 1980, 97-176; Clayman 1980, 72-83.

30. See Segal 2001, 20-2, on 'fescennine' verse.

31. Invective in a generic form in that it attacked social conventions – see Segal 1968, 7-14, where Segal puts Plautine comedy in context: as he phrases it, 'to a society with a fantastic compulsion for hierarchies, order, and obedience, he [Plautus] presents a saturnalian chaos' (13); also cf. Segal 2001, 183-204, for Plautus' comedy put in literary-historical context.

32. On Lucilius' personal attacks see Hor. *Sat.* 1.4.6; 2.1.62ff; Pers. 1.114-15. Yet R. Mayer, 'Friendship in the Satirists', in S.H. Braund (ed.), *Satire and Society in Ancient Rome; Exeter Studies in History No. 23* (Exeter 1989), 7-8, suggests that Lucilius' attacks were more on vices, where the named individuals were representative of that particular vice.

33. On Horace, Persius, and Juvenal sidestepping the issue of attacking individuals see Braund 1996, 116-21.

34. On Roman satirists' justifications for their invective see Spisak 1994b, 301-3.

35. On the irony of Horace's claim that he is not a poet see Oberhelman and Armstrong, 'Satire as Poetry and the Impossibility of Metathesis in Horace's *Satires*', in D. Obbink (ed.) *Philodemus and Poetry: Poetic Theory and Practice in Lucretius, Philodemus, and Horace* (New York 1995), 233ff.; and Freudenburg 1993, 124ff.

36. N. Rudd's poetic and highly effective rendering of the lines.

37. See Colton 1991.

38. Juv. 1.1-30, where, after slamming the writers of epic and tragedy and then listing a string of vices, he culminates with the famous line: *difficile est saturam non scribere*.

39. Juvenal's avowed personal inspiration is *indignatio*, a (moral) 'indignation' which he declares supplements whatever natural talent he has for writing (1.79-80).

40. For Martial's ties with satire see Mendell 1922, 20; Sullivan 1987, 259-65, who categorizes Martial as a 'social poet and an acute ... critic of contemporary Roman society' (260); also Sullivan 1991, 104-5, where he would include Martial in the tradition of Roman satire because he shares so much with the satirists; and Szelest 1986, 2584 with n. 40. Moreover, one could argue that Roman satire was a developed form of *vers de société*, a literary form with which Roman epigram had so much in common.

41. See further Spisak 1994b, 303-6, on Martial's justification of his genre at 8.3, 4.49, and 10.4.

42. Martial also attacks poetry on mythological themes at 4.49 and 9.50. Cf. Persius 5.14-20; Juvenal 1.4-21 for similar attacks. Also see Bramble 1974, 12-13, on the motif of 'the rejection of mythology' in the Roman poets.

43. On Martial's subject-matter, cf. Pliny's description of his own social verse: these poems 'comprise our loves and hatreds, our indignation, compassion and wit, in fact every phase of life and every detail of our public and professional activities' (Pliny *Ep.* 7.9.12-14).

44. About 55% of the poems of the twelve-book collection are invective (see above, where Szelest 1986, 2584, n. 40, is cited). As for Martial's justification for his poetry, which mostly centres on the invective, roughly 10% of the poems of the twelve-book collection (just over 100 poems) have to do with the poet's reflections on his own work (Holzberg 1988, 88). On these poems see Citroni, 1968; Holzberg 1988, 85-93; Sullivan 1991, 56-77 (a later version of Sullivan 1977).

45. I follow Henderson 1991, 2 for the definition of obscenity: verbal reference to sexual and excremental areas and activities that are taboo according to the prevailing social customs; on the Roman concept of obscenity see Richlin 1992, 1-31, to which I refer for what follows. On obscenity as part of the iambic tradition, see Henderson, 1991, 14-18, who notes that obscenity 'was proper to archaic blame, ... because it belonged to the primitive rituals from which iambic metres devolved ...'

46. For the sense of a 'clear conscience' see Howell 1980, ad loc.; and Citroni 1975, ad loc., who cites in support Juv. 1.165ff; cf. also Phaedrus 3 *prol.* 45-8. A passage from Horace's *Satire* 1.4 (1.4.65ff., cited by both Howell and Citroni) helps clarify Martial's meaning here: Horace, in justifying his satire against the charge of malice, says that if anyone lives well and with pure hands (*bene si quis et vivat puris manibus*), he or she has nothing to fear from those who have made it their business to go about broadcasting reprehensible behaviour. Horace uses the names of Caprius and Sulcius for such libel mongers; these men were apparently contemporary writers of satire (see B.L. Ullman, 'Horace and the Nature of Satire', *TAPA* 48 [1917]: 117-18).

47. On Domitian's prosecution of writers who libelled highly placed persons see Suet. *Dom.* 8.3. Martial's specific protest against other writers' improper use of verse – that is, controversial verse for which Martial would get the blame – is most strong in Book 1 with its six poems on plagiarism, but also echoes throughout the rest of the twelve-book collection. For example, Martial at 7.72.12-16 has the poet disavow verses 'dripping with black venom'; and at 10.3 he disavows 'quips of home-bred slaves, vulgar abuse, and the ugly railings of a vendor's tongue' that a certain anonymous poet scatters abroad under Martial's name; Martial's poet-persona declares in response, 'May black fame be far off from my books' (10.3.9).

48. Shackleton Bailey 1993 translates *verna* ('house-born slave') as equivalent to *scurra*, 'vulgar buffoon', because of the stereotype of the spoiled house-born slave who took liberties in speech and action (see further Post 1908, ad loc.). On the sense of *procacitas* as 'wantonness' cf. at 2.41.17, where the context gives it just that sense.

49. Cf. 7.12, where Martial states: 'So may our Lord [i.e. Domitian] read me with an untroubled brow, Faustinus, and catch my jokes with a favouring ear, since my page has not even harmed those it justly hates, and fame that comes from someone's blush does not please me'; also cf. 10.33.9-10, where Martial sums up neatly his programme of attack, so to speak, with his invective: 'This rule my little books know how to keep: to spare persons; to speak about vices.'

50. On 6.44 see Grewing 1997, 310-17; as noted by Grewing, Martial wittily pays back Calliodorus in kind by accusing him of *os impurum*, 'an unclean mouth' – i.e. of being a fellator, a most heinous charge against a Roman male. For the *scurra* in Martial's poems see Damon 1997, 146-71.

51. Martial's condemnation of the undiscriminating joker is in line with Aristotle's condemnation of the βωμόλοχος, the 'buffoon', in his theory of the liberal jest (*Eth. Nic.* 4.1127b33-1128b4/4.8.1-11, on which see Freudenburg 1993, 55-6).

52. On *latine loqui*, 'to speak in plain Latin', cf. *Priap.* 3.9-10, *Latine / dicere*, with the same sense. For a listing of words ancient Romans considered obscene see Richlin 1992, 18-30; Richlin (25-6) gives these general characteristics for the primary obscenities: (1) they are not used as expletives; (2)

they often have their full sexual meaning; (3) the concept of dirt and befoulment with dirt is commonly associated with them and so they are conceived as intrinsically foul; (4) they are delimited – i.e. an out-of-place context makes words obscene (e.g. *futuo, -ere*, 'fuck', is acceptable as part of a mime performance, but not in oratory).

53. On the sexual connotation for *ludere* in Martial see Spisak, 1992, 49-50; on *iocus* see Spisak 1992, 179-80, with n. 17, and Grewing 1997, 529; and for *lusus* see Spisak 1992, 182 with n. 20.

54. Martial used most of his obscene language in his invective: the majority in attacks on those who are involved in abnormal sexual acts (e.g. oral sex; passive homosexuality; adultery) – see Watson and Watson 2003, 22.

55. Martial's works contain more obscenity than the extant works of any other Roman writer – see Adams 1982, 218-25, for a survey of obscenity in Latin literature. Moreover, it seems that more readers have taken offence at Martial's use of obscenity and his graphic sexual content than at anything else – e.g. in the collection Sullivan put together of criticism of Martial's poetry through the ages, complaints about Martial's obscenity and sexual content appear most frequently and are most vociferous (Sullivan 1993, 73-233).

56. Cf. 10.64, where Martial cites the obscenity of Lucan's poems as a precedent.

57. On the idea in ancient times that a person's character is reflected in his literary style see Richlin1992, 3-5; also cf. Ov. *Trist.* 2.354.

58. See 1.4.8: *lasciva est nobis pagina, vita proba*: 'my page is wanton, my life upright'; and 11.15: *mores non habet hic meos libellus*: 'this little book does not have my morals'.

59. On this topos, cf. Martial 1.35.12-13; 4.14.11-12; 11.2; 11.16; 11.20.1-2; also see Richlin 1992, 5-7.

60. Martial also uses *tristis* with a similar connotation at 1.3.10 of the stylus the poet uses to edit out (risqué) jokes; at 10.18.3 where he uses the phrase *nec tristia carmina* of his Saturnalian verse; and at 11.20.2, again of a reader unable to tolerate plain Latin. On *severus* see at 1.35 below. On *gravis* in a similar context see at 8.3.17, where it is linked with *severus* and used of poets who write tragedy and epic poetry fit for classroom recitation; and at 11.16.1, also of the reader unable to tolerate risqué verse; cf. Schöffel 2002, 72.

61. See Richlin 1992, 8-10, who cites Ovid *Ars Am.* 1.25-34 and *Priapea* 2 as well as several passages from Martial as examples of the poet justifying his poetry's obscene element by marking its 'quasi-religious boundaries' (8), boundaries that separate it from other poetry and give it special licence.

62. The Floralia were annual games, founded around 238 BCE and made annual in 173 BCE, which in Martial's day lasted six days (28 April – 3 May); they were held in honour of Flora, an old Italian goddess of flowering plants; see *RE* 6₂ 2749-52 (Wissowa); Howell 1980, 100; Richlin 1992, 10 and 228-9, n. 8; Gaffney 1976, 27-9; see also Ov. *Fast.* 4.943; 5.349; Lactant. *Div. Inst.* 1.20.7-10; Sen. *Ep.* 97.8; Val. Max. 2.10.8; S.H.A. 6.5. Martial also compares his epigrams to mime at 1.4.5-6; 3.86; 1.35.8-9; and 8 *praefatio* 10-14. On

Roman mime see R.E. Fantham, 'Mime: The Missing Link in Roman Literary History', *CW* 82.3 (1989): 153-63.

63. See Introduction for the development of 'literary iambus' through the inspiration Archilochus received from his part in Demeter's festive rituals that involved ritual and abusive jesting. Cf. Richlin 1992, 10, who in speaking specifically of the *ludi Florales*, triumphs, and the Saturnalia says: 'the *apologiae* in Roman sexual poetry are announcements by the poets that the obscenity in their work is to be aligned with such celebrations.'

64. On the Roman triumph, see most conveniently Richlin 1992, 10 and 229, n. 9; on the *thalassio* see at 1.35.6-7 below; on the Saturnalia, see at 11.15 and also Ch. 4.

65. E.g. 9.28.3; 11.2.1-2; cf. Petron. *Sat.* 132.15.

66. The Cato story appears in Valerius Maximus' handbook of rhetorical examples (2.10.8); it is also cited by Seneca *Ep.* 97.7.

67. Cf. Richlin 1992, 7, on this closing four-line poem: 'With a typical epigrammatic twist, Martial insinuates that any who criticize [his poems' obscenity and sexual content] are just going out of their way to be shocked, to call attention to themselves.'

68. Martial several times characterizes his verse as suitable for the Saturnalia – see 4.14.6-12, 5.30, 7.28, 10.18, 11.2, 11.6, 11.15, 13.1, 14.1. Statius likewise characterizes his light verse as suitable for the Saturnalia at *Silv.* 1.6.1-8 and 93, where he bids Apollo and Minerva to depart from the festivities, and then asks Saturn, December (personified) along with its wine, and laughing jokes and bold witticisms to be present – on this poem see Newlands 2002, 227-59.

69. See Kay 1985, 1, for the date of the book and its association with the Saturnalia and Nerva.

70. See Kay 1985, 98-9, ad loc. on the Sabine women.

71. See Kay 1985, 69, at line 2 for Numa.

72. For a more direct statement of the connection between the obscenity and explicit sexual content of Martial's verse and the licence of the Saturnalia see: 4.14.12 where he describes his poems written for the Saturnalia as 'books steeped in wanton jokes' (*lacivis madidos iocis libellos*); 7.28.8 where he describes them as 'jokes' (*ioci*); 10.18.3, where he again calls them 'jokes', and also 'not sad poems' (10.18.3); 11.6 , where he plays around with his verse (*versu ludere*, line 3) within a sexual context (see Kay 1985, 75-6, on line 15); and 11.15 where he personifies the book, which is specifically released for the Saturnalia, as laughing, 'naughtier' than all his others, soaked in wine and perfume, able to play (with sexual overtone) with the boys and love the girls, and to use obscenity.

73. On the licence of the Saturnalia see Leary 2001, 5-6. For a full description of the Saturnalia, see Ch. 4, where its connection with Martial's conception of the good life is discussed.

74. See Macrob. *Sat.* 2.1.8-9, where the Saturnalian dinner party company decides to forego the usual improper and indecent after-dinner jokes for a selection of jokes from famous men of old, some of which, however, are at least as risqué as some of Martial's – e.g. those involving Julia, daughter of Augustus (Macrob. *Sat.* 2.5).

75. Nauta 2002, 166-89 and esp. 187, makes the case very well for Martial's books as Saturnalian gifts.

76. The Saturnalia fell between two other harvest-related festivals (the *Consualia* in honour of Consus, the god of the corn bin, and the *Opalia*, in honour of Ops, a personification of abundance) – see further Versnel 1993, 143; also on Saturn's connection with sowing and harvesting and the significance of the time of the festival see Scullard 1981, 205-6; Leary 2001, 4. Versnel 1993, 164-84, argues that the festival marks the opening of the new grain stores.

77. On the universal use of invective and obscenity to avert evil spirits and promote fertility see Segal 2001, 19-21, with n. 63 (on p. 240) – Segal aptly calls it 'the curse that blesses' (20); also see Richlin 1992, 10 (with n. 11): in speaking of the *ludi Florales*, triumphs, and the Saturnalia Richlin states, 'Such festivals of reversal, many involving obscenity, are found in all societies, and their function is to ward off evil from those in power (as in a triumph) and increase fertility (as in the *ludi Florales*).'

78. Mikhail Bakhtin's theory of the carnivalesque seems to apply and support this interpretation of Martial's obscene Saturnalian invective as a liberating and revitalizing force. As a festival of reversal, the Saturnalia qualifies as a species of Bakhtin's carnival (see Bakhtin 1984a, 129, where Bakhtin calls the Roman Saturnalia the 'central festival of the carnival type'): among other things, Bakhtin's carnival includes the element of 'profanation', which he describes as carnivalistic blasphemies, debasings, 'bringings down to earth', and 'carnivalistic obscenities linked with the reproductive power of the earth and the body' (Bakhtin 1984a, 123). The laughter produced by these profanations was always, Bakhtin maintains, directed toward something higher, either a god or 'the highest earthy authority', where the shame and ridicule forced them to renew themselves; moreover, Bakhtin maintains that 'all forms of ritual laughter were linked with death and rebirth, with the reproductive acts, with symbols of the reproductive force' (Bakhtin 1984a 126-7). See Ch. 4 for more on Bakhtin's carnival as applied to Martial's conception of the good life.

79. On *severus* cf. line 12 of this epigram, *deposita severitas*, 'with your austerity put aside'; 1 *praef.* 24, of Cato; 3.20.6, of a writer of epic poetry; 4.14.6, of the epic poet Silius Italicus; 8 *praef.* 11, of distinguished men (who have nonetheless written licentious verse); 8.3.17, *nimium severi*, of those who write verse fit for recitation in schools; 10.20.1, *parum severus* of Martial's tenth book; 11.2.1, of Cato's brow expressing disapproval of Martial's Saturnalian verse (on which see above). On *gravis* and *tristis* see above at 1 *praef.*

80. Such phallic imagery for obscenity and sexual content is not unique here: see also 3.68; 3.69; 11.15; and *Priapea* 1.7-8; 2.6-8. For specific interpretations of 1.35 and other of these passages see Williams 2002, 161-6; also see J.P. Hallett, '*Nec castrare velis meos libellos.* Sexual and Poetic *Lusus* in

Catullus, Martial and the *Carmina Priapea*', in C. Klodt (ed.), *Satura Lanx: Festschrift fur Werner A. Krenkel zum 70* (Hildesheim 1996), 326ff.

81. See Segal 2001, 17-20, for the phallus as 'a symbol and instrument not only for the continuity of the species, but for the flowering of the fields as well' (18).

82. Cf. Catull. 61.127, where *Talassio* is used in the context of *Fescennini*, ribald and obscene taunts in verse, which were a regular accompaniment of the Roman marriage ceremony (on *Fescennini* see *RE* 6_2.222-3). Moreover, according to Livy (1.9.12) and Plutarch (*Quaest. Rom.* 31, *Rom.* 15) this public ritual for the encouragement of begetting children had deeper significance: these two sources connect the *thalassio* invocation to one Thalassius, a person who, for the occasion of the kidnapping of the Sabine women, sent men to carry off one of the most beautiful of the Sabine women for himself. Thus, this *thalassio* invocation had its origin in an officially sanctioned act to increase the population.

83. Strabo 13.1.12 and Pausanias 9.31.2 for Priapus' parents. The fullest account for Priapus is H. Herter, *De Priapo. Religionsgeschichtliche Versuche und Vorarbeiten* 23 (Giessen 1932); also see Herter's accounts in *RE* and *Der Kleine Pauly* (1974 edn); also O'Connor 1989, 18-42.

84. See Richlin 1992, passim, for Priapus in Roman literature; for Priapus in ancient literature in general, see O'Connor 1989, 26-42.

85. O'Connor 1989, 24.

86. O'Connor 1989, 33; and Richlin 1992, 58: Richlin in her book-length study of ancient Roman humour portrays Priapus in the literature as a minatory figure that 'stands at the centre of the whole complex of Roman sexual humour. The general stance of this figure is that of a threatening male. He is anxious to defend himself by adducing his strength, virility, and (in general) all traits that are considered normal ...' Cf. Martial 6.16; 6.72; 6.73; 7.91; 8.40.

87. On *Gallus* see *RE* 7_1.674-82; cf. Mart. 2.45.2, with commentary by Williams 2004, 166; also Martial 9.2.13; 11.72; 11.74.

88. E.g. at 10.92.11-12 Martial has him as a pursuer of none other than Flora, the old Italian vegetation goddess; cf. also 7.91, where Priapus is portrayed as lusting after wanton girls; at 6.16, where he allows boys and lovely girls to enter his garden; or even 11.51, simply for the size of his phallus.

89. O'Connor 1989, 33: 'In post-Augustan literature Priapus functioned as the traditional *custos hortorum*, a buffoonish wooden god and a burlesque of a traditional deity.'

90. Newman 1990, 72, in his characterization of Catullus as an iambographer, addresses this aspect of Catullus – what Newman terms 'the "nugatory" aspect of the Roman genius'. This term 'nugatory' comes from the Latin word *nugae*, 'trifles', which term Catullus used of his poetry in his opening poem (and which Martial frequently uses of his own poetry). Newman defines *nugae* as: 'the personification and resurrection of the irrational, dark, stupid, childish, obscene, rejected, dead side of experience which is yet so strong in its humility that it can challenge the conventionally wise and lay low the mighty. But not to destroy! Rather to restore wholeness and unity to our fragmented and partial mentalities' (40).

2. *Amicitia*

1. On *vers de société*, 'social verse', see Ch. 1.

2. Certain scholars have construed Martial's frequent attention to reciprocity as a preoccupation with the simple acquisition of goods and services – something typical of a patron-client relationship – e.g. Post 1908, xiii, characterizes Martial as 'a chronic beggar'. Usually, and actually more damningly, Martial's persona is automatically regarded as a client to his wealthy patronlike addressees without any or much regard for social conditions. For a chronological range of criticism of Martial (beginning with Martial's comments on himself), almost all of which presents Martial's persona as a traditional client, see Sullivan 1993, 69-233.

3. See Konstan 1997, 1-3, for friendship as an 'historical variable'.

4. See Konstan 1997, 3-6, on the anthropological approach and its influence on Finley.

5. Konstan 1997, 4-5, who conjectures that the roots of this thesis may be found in the social theories of the eighteenth-century liberal Scots thinkers (e.g. Adam Ferguson, David Hume).

6. For a definition of social reciprocity in anthropological theory see H. van Wees, 'The Law of Gratitude: Reciprocity in Anthropological Theory', in Gill, Postlethwaite, and Seaford 1998, 13-49.

7. On the consensus that ancient friendship was based on obligatory reciprocity instead of affection and generosity see Konstan 1997, 5.

8. The workings and objectives of social reciprocity are well attested by both the ancient Greeks and Romans, e.g. Homer, Aristotle, Cicero, Seneca: for details on Homeric gift-giving see A.J. Finley, *The World of Odysseus* (New York 1954; rev. edn 1978), 64-6, 120-3; J.T. Fitzgerald (ed.), *Graeco-Roman Perspectives on Friendship* (Atlanta, GA 1997), 13-34; on the ideology of the ancient Greek practice of gift-giving and reciprocity see Kurke 1991, 85-107; and P. Millett, *Lending and Borrowing in Ancient Athens* (Cambridge 1991), 27-44; on reciprocity in ancient Greece see Gill, Postlethwaite, and Seaford 1998; I. Morris, 'Gift and Commodity in Archaic Greece', *Man* 21 (1986): 1-17; for a general survey treatment of instances of ancient Greek and Roman social reciprocity see Hands 1968, 26-35; on reciprocity specifically in Martial, see Spisak 1998.

9. κατ' ἰσότητα δεῖ τῷ φιλεῖ καὶ τοῖς λοιποῖς ἰσάζειν (*Eth. Nic.* 1162b2-4/8.13.1).

10. See E. Flaig, 'Loyalität ist keine Gefälligkeit: Zum Majestätsprozeß gegen C. Silius 24 n. Chr', *Klio* 75 (1993): 299-304, esp. 299-300 for the contrast between Hellenic (and also Semitic) and Roman social reciprocity, and how unique and indispensable it was to Roman society.

11. Sen. *de Ben.*; also cf. Sen. *Ep. 81*, which is a more succinct treatment of the protocol of giving and receiving kindnesses.

12. [...] quae maxime humanam societatem alligat (*de Ben.* 1.4.2). Erunt homicidae, tyranni, fures, adulteri, raptores, sacrilegi, proditores; infra omnia ista ingratus est, nisi quod omnia ista ab ingrato sunt, sine quo vix ullum magnum facinus adcrevit (*de Ben.* 1.10.4). Cf. Cic. *Off.* 1.48, where he says that a good man is not permitted to fail to repay favours.

13. Cf. Konstan 1997, 127: 'Seneca ... exhaustively analyzes expectations of return on loans and favors, but rarely raises the subject of friendship.'

14. See Arist. *Eth. Nic.* 1156a-1156b33/8.2.4-8.3.9.

15. ... a natura ... potius quam indigentia orta amicitia, applicatione magis animi cum quodam sensu amandi, quam cogitatione quantum illa res utilitatis esset habitura (Cic., *de Amic.* 27).

16. Quam si putant ab imbecillitate proficisci, ut sit per quem adsequatur quod quisque desideret, humilem sane relinquunt et minime generosum ... ortum amicitiae, quam ex inopia atque indigentia natam volunt (Cic., *de Amic.* 29).

17. See Konstan 1997, passim, whose main thesis is that the ancients did have, contrary to prevailing scholarly opinion, the equivalent of modern day friendship: he argues that friendship in the classical world was 'a personal relationship predicated on affection and generosity rather than on obligatory reciprocity' (5).

18. Arist. *Eth. Nic.* 1156b25ff./8.3.8; Cic. *de Amic.* 20.

19. As Peter Brunt (Brunt 1988, 381) put it, who with his definition was reacting to the early twentieth-century narrow conception of *amicitia* as 'the good old word for [political] party relationships' (L.R. Taylor, *Party Politics in the Age of Caesar* [1949], 7) or Ronald Syme's equation of *amicitia* with *factio*, a 'political faction' (R. Syme, *Roman Revolution* [1939], 157): 'The range of *amicitia* was vast. From the constant intimacy and goodwill of virtuous or at least like-minded men to the courtesy that etiquette normally enjoined on gentlemen, it covers every degree of genuinely or overtly amicable relation.'

20. See Saller 1982, 12, as quoted above, previous section, for the summation of the inherent paradox of ancient friendship. Cf. Michel 1962, 502-29 (as cited by Saller 1982, 13, n. 29), who stresses the two lines of thought on friendship of the Latin moralists: (1) a pragmatic, reciprocal exchange, which was pervasive in society, and (2) a selfless, spiritual friendship. Cf. also Verboven 2002, 45, on *amicitia* as a complex relationship 'in which reciprocity, affection and personal loyalty were mingled and advantage and altruism intertwined, together producing and being produced by *beneficia*.'

21. For this definition of *colo, colere* see the *OLD*, s.v., 7b. Cf. Martial's use of *colo, -ere* at 3.38.11; 6.50.1; 12.68.2, all usages of people seeking to benefit materially from their association with the wealthy; also cf. Cic. *de Amic.* 69; Sen. *Ep.* 47.18; *Laus Pisonis* 113; Statius *Silv.* 1.4.36; Pliny *Ep.* 7.31.5; Iuv. 7.37, all examples of *colere* marking a social distinction of rank.

22. On the sense of *regnum, regni* as 'patronage' cf. Martial's usage of *rex*, *regis* for 'patron' in this same poem (line 9), and also at 1.112.1; 2.18.5&8; 2.68.2; 3.7.5; 4.83.5; 5.22.14; 10.10.5; 10.96.13; 12.60.14; also Iuv. 5.14; 7.45; *OLD* s.v., 8. Pisos refers to the family of Gaius Calpurnius Piso, the figurehead of the conspiracy against Nero in 65 CE. The house of Seneca is here called *ter numeranda*, 'thrice distinguished', because of its three most distinguished members: the elder Seneca ('Rhetor'), the younger Seneca (the philosopher), and the younger Seneca's nephew, Lucan (see Shackleton Bailey 1993 ad loc.); cf. 12.36.

23. See White 1978, 79-80 (but cf. Saller 1982, 10 for the qualification that inscriptions not infrequently used the term *patronus* with the sense of 'patron', as we understand it). When Martial did use the terms *patronus* and *cliens* he specifically used them to signify: (1) the relation between an orator (i.e. advocate) and his legal client (1.97.2; 1.98.2; 2.13.1; 2.27.2; 4.46.12; 4.88.4; 7.72.14; 8.33.12; 8.76.4); (2) the relation between an ex-master and his freedman (1.101.9; 5.34.7; 5.70.1; 6.28.3; 6.29.3; 9.73.3; 10.34.3; 12.49.6); and (3) the relation between a person who seeks to attach himself to a wealthy person as a satellite (1.49.33; 7.62.4; 7.63.8; 9.2.10; 9.22.10; 10.10.11; 10.34.5; 10.74.2; 10.87.5; 12.68.2; 12.77.6). On the general usage of both these terms see Nauta 2002, 11-15; White 1978, 79-80; 1993, 30-1; on early and Republican *clientela* see Brunt 1988, 382-442 and Hellegourc'h 1963, 54-6; on the terms *patronus* and *cliens* in the early Empire see Saller 1982, 8-11. On *rex* for 'patron' see above; on *dominus* as 'patron' see 2.68.2; 4.83.5; 10.10.5; 12.60.14.

24. Terms most favoured by Martial are *amicus, amicitia, amor* and *amare*, and especially *sodalis*; and the first person possessive adjectives *meus* and *noster* (see esp. Nauta 2002, 14-18; White 1978, 79-82; Hellegourc'h 1963, 42ff., 142ff. on the use of these terms).

25. See White 1978, 80; and 1993, 27-30 for the formally undefined nature of most friendships; White estimates at 20% references where friendship was characterized as other than between equals (1993, 29). On the nature of *amicitia* in general, see Konstan 1997, 122-48; and L. Pizzolato, *L'idea di amicizia* (Torino 1993), 89-213; for the Republican conception see Brunt 1988, 351-81; B. Fiore, 'The Theory and Practice of Friendship in Cicero', in J.T. Fitzgerald (ed.), *Greco-Roman Perspectives on Friendship* (Atlanta, GA 1997), 59-76; for the similar early Empire conception of *amicitia*, see R. Seager, '*Amicitia* in Tacitus and Juvenal', *AJAH* 2 (1977): 40-50. For the view that grades of friendship were more distinct see Saller 1982, 11-15; 1983, 255-6; Garnsey and Saller 1997, 97, where they cite Pliny, *Ep.* 7.3.2, 2.6.2; Seneca, *Ep.* 94.14.

26. See, e.g., Cic. *Fam.* 9.20.3 for *amici* performing the *salutatio*. In general, for the services Roman *amici* provided to each other see Saller 1982, 119-43; 1989, 57-61; White 1993, 14-27.

27. On Sextus Julius Frontinus see *OCD*; *RE* 243. He had a long and distinguished political career: he served as praetor (70 CE); consul in 72 or 73; governor of Britain (73/74-7); proconsul of Asia (86); *curator aquarum* (97); suffect consul (98); consul (100). Pliny described him as one of the two most distinguished men of his day (*Ep.* 5.1). His writing was on the history, administration, and maintenance of the aqueducts (*de Aquis urbis Romae*); also he wrote on techniques of military command (the *Strategemata*); on military science (now lost); and on land-surveying (partially preserved in the *Corpus Agrimensorum*).

28. Cf. Post 1908, 260 at 10.58.14, where he assesses the poet as a client.

29. The term 'patronage' does not come by way of the Latin nouns *patrocinium* or *patronatus*; rather it was a new coinage of French. Thus it was bound to have picked up new connotations over the centuries – White 1993, 32-3; for a detailed etymological history of the term see White 1978, 78-80. However, Nauta 2002, 11-34 (see especially 14-18), disputes White's rejection of the term patronage because the use of *amicus* does not differentiate between the various kinds of relationships that the Romans called *amicitia* – some of which were obviously between a patron and client. Rather, Nauta 2002, 18-26, defines much more precisely what is meant by patronage (and literary patronage) as based on Saller's sociological sense of the term: the relationship must be voluntary, must not be subject to legal regulation, must be asymmetrical, must be personal and of some duration, and must involve the reciprocal exchange of goods and services. My use of the theory of social exchange to analyse Martial's treatment of *amicitia* – see next section on 'Social exchange' – coincides well with Nauta's definition.

30. White 1982, 58; also see White 1993, 32-4. E.g., according to White's literary-historical study of the relationship between Roman poets and their wealthy friends (White 1993, 3-34, and originally 1978, 74-92), of the Roman poets from 40 BCE to 140 CE, senators and knights constituted at the very least 55% of those poets of whose verse any trace remains, and more likely up to as high as 94%.

31. 'Gifts as hooks' poems having to do with *captatio* (or dowry-hunting) are 1.10; 2.40; 4.56; 5.39; 6.62; 6.63; 8.27; 9.8(9); 9.48; 11.44; 11.55; 11.67; 11.83; 12.40; 12.90; cf. 8.38; Pliny *Ep.* 9.30.2.

32. On gifts given as bait or in the wrong spirit see also 5.59, where Martial writes: '*quisquis magna dedit, voluit sibi magna remitti*'; likewise cf. 8.38.1-3; and Pliny *Ep.* 9.30.2.

33. On *vetus sodalis* see Williams 2004, 120-1.

34. The pioneers of the theory of social exchange are: G.C. Homans, 'Social Behavior as Exchange', *American Journal of Sociology* 63 (1958): 597-606; G.C. Homans, *Social Behavior: Its Elementary Forms* (New York 1961; rev. edn 1974), 30-72, who is usually given credit for the first systematic modern theory of social exchange; Thibaut and Kelley, *The Social Psychology of Groups* (New York 1959), 9-99; and Blau 1964, 88-114, and 1974, 204-14. The pivotal anthropological work on social reciprocity, to which both Homans and Blau refer in formulating their own theories, is M. Mauss, *The Gift: The Form and Reason for Exchange in Archaic Societies*, trans. by I. Cunnison (London; first published in 1925 as *Essai sur le don, forme et raison de l'échange dans les sociétés archaïques* in *Année Sociologie*, n.s., 1 (1925): 30-186; cf. also, as a pivotal study for social exchange theory, A.W. Gouldner, 'The Norm of Reciprocity: A Preliminary Statement', *American Sociological Review* 25.2 (1960): 161-78.

35. Blau 1974, 207; also Blau 1964, 88, where Blau starts his chapter on social exchange by quoting from Aristotle's *Nicomachean Ethics*, 1162b31-1163a1/8.13.7-9.

36. Blau 1974, 207. The passage cited is Arist. *Eth. Nic.* 1162b31-34/8.13.7.

37. Blau 1974, 204. For the explanation of social exchange which follows, see most conveniently Blau 1974, 204-14 (except when noted otherwise).

38. Blau 1974, 212, distinguishes between a power-exchange and mutual social exchange: in the power-exchange the original giver determines when return will be made; in the mutual exchange the recipient of the gift determines when return will be made.

39. On the effects of Roman *infamia*, social disgrace which results from default in the social exchange, see Michel 1962, 589. The arrangement between Roman orators (advocates) and those they represented, their (legal) clients, is a good example of the informal contract in Roman social exchange: orators up until the late first century CE were by law not permitted to collect fees or gifts above a certain value from their clients (the *lex Cincia*, on which see E. Baltrusch, *Regimen morum: Die Reglementierung des Privatlebens der Senatoren und Ritter in der römischen Republik und frühen Kaiserzeit* (= Vestigia 41) (Munich 1989), 63ff. Clients, however, were still expected to recompense their advocates with some gift or service, and failure to do so brought social castigation (cf., e.g., Martial epigram 1.98).

40. One explanation is that altruistic acts are actually in exchange for altruistically motivated benefits received in the past – e.g. the sort of service academics perform when writing references for junior colleagues (see J.K. Chadwick-Jones, *Social Exchange Theory: Its Structure and Influence in Social Psychology* [London, 1976], 251-2).

41. Blau 1974, 208-210, where Blau distinguishes between social and economic exchange; also see Blau 1964, 93-5.

42. Putnam 2000, 18-24, for the definition; on 19-20 Putnam tracks the history of the term.

43. Gold 2003, 601.

44. On the sense of *fides* see Verboven 2002, 39-41, who says that its 'original meaning seems to have been "trust", both in an active sense – the trust put in someone – and in the passive sense – the trust enjoyed by someone and hence the disposition deserving of trust. This trust is based on loyalty and solidarity, manifest in the acknowledgment of personal obligations (*officia*)'; as he terms it, *fides* 'served as the cement of personal relations' and as such 'was the true core of Roman friendship'; he cites as support Freyburger 1986, passim, and Hellegourc'h 1963, 23-5.

45. Sen. *Ben.* 6.3.3, and cf. 6.3.1, both as cited by Verboven 2002, 64, n. 13; also cf. Michel 1962, 522 (also cited by Verboven 2002, 64, n. 13).

46. Cic. *Rosc. Am.* 111-12; as noted by Konstan 1997, 130. Cf. E. Baltrusch,

Regimen morum: Die Reglementierung des Privatlebens der Senatoren und Ritter in der römischen Republik und frühen Kaiserzeit, Vestigia 41 (Munich 1989), 64-5, where in comment on the *lex Cincia* he says that *fides* was a prerequisite for the functioning of the whole (as he terms it) patron-client system.

47. Cf. Kurke 1991, 94, on gift exchange: 'gift giving is not merely a material transaction but also a way of binding giver and receiver together. Far more important than their functional value as objects, gifts connect people and groups: they create community.'

48. E.g. Post 1908, 143, terms the poem 'a polite and artful beggar's plea'.

49. Cf. Gold 2003, 612, who says, in speaking of Martial's many poems on patronage, 'We see in them a writer who moves from the commodification and objectification of gifts to the subtler nuances of the process of a gift-exchange culture, creating as he goes a philosophy of giving.'

50. See Hoffer 1999, 11-12, on the great value of symbolic capital.

51. Blau 1974, 206. Moreover, Blau's second general function of social exchange, 'to establish superordination over others' (Blau 1964, 89), is particularly apropos of ancient Roman culture in that for the highly status-conscious Romans the ability to provide goods and services to friends was a relatively safe and sure way to increase one's power and prestige, as well as access to services – see further in the next chapter. Hands 1968, 34-5, posits that the very wealthy man could do little else with his money than invest it in friends. Saller 1982, 126, notes the absence in Roman society of the capitalistic spirit because the capitalistic mentality was 'antithetical to and hindered by patronal values which encourage the utilization of wealth primarily as a means of social domination in personal relationships'.

3. Poems of Praise

1. According to my own count, Martial's twelve-book collection contains 318 approbative poems and prose epistles. See Ward 1973, 128, for praise as part of the Indo-European poet-singer tradition; specifically, he cites the Rig-Veda 3.33.7, where it says that poet-singers had a dual function: 'to praise those in song who were worthy and to demean and lampoon others'. On praise as part of the ancient Greek iambic tradition see Burnett 1983, 25-6, with n. 25, on Archilochus writing paeans for Apollo and other gods; also Archilochus was named as the first to give the ritual invocation of Heracles that brought him into every victory at Olympia at the games – cf. Pindar *Ol.* 9.1-4 and Archilochus fr. 324 (Gerber).

2. See White, 1975, on many of these persons Martial praises; also Nauta 2002, 148-66, for the major players; on the historical figures see A. Nordh, 'Historical *exempla* in Martial', *Eranos* 52 (1954): 224-38. Most studies assume that for the most part the poet-persona of the poems of praise represents Martial himself and that the poems' honorands are likewise representations of historical persons – see Nauta 2002, 39-58, on making this determination for Martial's poems to patrons; as Nauta phrases it, he sees Martial as performing speech acts with his poems to patrons instead of representing speech acts (48). Other studies, however – notably Fowler 1995 and Lorenz 2002 (in his treatment of the poems to or on the emperors) – posit that the poet-persona and/or honorands are better taken as literary constructs, completely or in part: i.e. Martial is representing speech acts with his poems to patrons instead of performing them. My own approach follows Nauta: Martial performs speech acts (instead of representing them), although it incorporates some representation of speech acts, too; see further below for details.

3. E.g. E.T. Salmon, *A History of the Roman World from 30 BC to AD 138* (London 1959) 266: Martial has been perceived as an 'unlovely character who courted the favours of the great with the grossest flattery'; also Post, 1908, xxxi, in the introduction to his commentary on Martial says of him: 'when he is thinking of the emperor or his minions he is a consummate lickspittle and time-serving hypocrite'. Further examples of criticism of Martial as hypocritical and self-serving in his praise of Domitian through the ages can be found in Sullivan 1993, 80; 135; 135-6; 190-1; 203.

4. For the various proponents of the basic views, see Lorenz 2002, 42-50; also Nauta 2002, 412-30, for an exposition and refutation of scholarship on Martial's and Statius' panegyric as containing a subversive subtext; cf. the remarks of Geyssen 1996, 6 (on the Statius' imperial panegyrics), who notes the same bipolar view of Statius' treatment of Domitian; Geyysen also notes the recent tendency, which is in reaction to a seeming inconsistency of praise for a bad emperor, 'to see all of Flavian literature as some type of criticism' (14, n. 32) – this also applies to scholarship on Martial.

5. See Burnett 1983, 55: '... archaic poetry of blame was an instrument of social health, as necessary to a sound community as those complementary songs [i.e. poems of praise] that put splendour in the air.' Burnett goes on to say that abuse was 'one of the two poetic practices essential to social life' (55), with praise poetry understood to be the other poetical practice to which she refers; also see Nagy 1976, 196, who cites Pindar fr. 181S in support of praise and invective as 'two sides of the same thing'; and Gentili 1988, 107-8 (with notes), who notes that in Sparta (as gleaned from Plutarch *Lyc.* 8.3; 25.3) praise and blame were 'even integrated into the institutional system, functioning specifically to further the greater good of the community by praising the worthy and censuring the unworthy'.

6. A point especially brought to my awareness by W.T. Gallwey, *The Inner Game of Tennis* (New York 1974), 43, where, in support of his own contention that any positive reaction to behaviour is just as much a form of control as criticism, he quotes this comment from one of his students in tennis: 'Compliments are criticisms in disguise'.

7. Conversely, the blame poet, through his sometimes obscene jokes and ridicule, caused divisiveness and a covert questioning of self, and was a potential threat to anyone in power. As Burnett 1983, 58, puts it, blame poetry 'acted as a kind of popular review ... that any man who gained prominence would have to undergo. Its power could even be projected into the future with an inhibitory effect.'

8. Martial's so-called poeticizing is nothing more than the incorporation of literary topoi, including myth and legend, or notable treatments of a subject or theme by other authors; his own elaborations upon these topoi and typical treatments as applied to his praise of individuals are what makes his own poems unique and inspired – see, e.g., Pitcher 1998, 59-76, and also S. Hinds, *Allusion and Intertext* (Cambridge 1998), 129-35, on Martial's use of Ovid; see R. Paukstadt, *De Martiale Catulli imitatore* (Diss., Halle, 1876) on his use of Catullus; cf. Holzberg 2002, 97-109, on Martial's *Intertexualität* (with bibliography for the section on 120-1).

9. Decianus is mentioned at 1.8, where he is praised for not taking Stoic principles too far; at 1.61.10 he is named Martial's compatriot and also an author; he is addressed at 1.24, which is an attack on Stoic hypocrites; and Book 2 is dedicated to him (2 *praef.*).

10. On Decianus see Howell 1980, 125. See this volume Ch. 4 on the *vir bonus* ideal, upon which Martial in good part builds his concept of the good life: the *vir bonus* it is characterized by honesty and a lack of guile, as well as integrity. Also hypocrisy is one of Martial's favourite targets for his invective (see Ch. 3).

11. See Grewing 1997, 196-7 at lines 5-7, for the warning as a topos.

12. E.g. 5.28, 6.54, 6.78, 7.14, 11.38, 12.51; on Aulus Pudens see M. Citroni, 'La carriera del centurione A. Pudens e il rango sociale dei primipilari', *Maia* 34 (1982): 247-57.

13. For examples of such charges see W. Fitzgerald, *Agonistic Poetry: The Pindaric Mode In Pindar, Horace, Hölderin, and the English Ode* (Berkeley 1987), 19 and 25, with n. 13.

14. See Woodbury 1968, 536, who in support cites W. Schmid, *Geschichte der griechischen Literatur* 1.1 (Munich 1929), 498, with n. 3; also A. Carson, *Economy of the Unlost: Reading Simonides of Keos with Paul Celan* (Princeton 1999), 15; and Gold 2003, 600.

15. See Woodbury 1968, 536, with n. 13, who cites the schol. on *Ol.* 1.1b; *Pyth.* 2.125a; 3.195a; *Nem.* 7.25a; *Isthm.* 5.2a. Also the subject of Woodbury's article, *Isthm.* 2.1-13, is used by critics to suggest a mercenary side of Pindar (see Woodbury 1968, 530); and Kurke 1991, 7 with n. 24.

16. See Kurke 1991, 135-59, her chapter on Pindar as a guest-friend to his object of praise; also Woodbury 1968, 537, with n. 14: for Pindar as a guest-friend to his so-called patrons Woodbury cites as examples *Ol.* 2.6, 4.15, 9.83; *Pyth.* 10.64; *Nem.* 7.61, 9.2; *Isthm.* 2.39 and 2.48.

17. Kurke 1991, 88-107, for the gift-exchange economy; 165-7, 249 for the terms 'embedded' and 'disembedded', which are from K. Polanyi, *Primitive, Archaic, and Modern Economies: Essays of Karl Polanyi*, ed. G. Dalton (Garden City, NY 1968), 81-2. For a precise summary of the two types of economy, see Gold 2003, 598-9.

18. Kurke 1991, 255-6; also 260 for a summary of the process.

19. On the paideutic function of Pindar's epinikia see Kurke 1991, 255, with n. 40. To those who are part of capitalistic societies this concept of the producer teaching or helping consumers to spend their money in the best way is almost impossible to conceive. We are inevitably suspicious. Perhaps the best analogue for Pindar's teaching of his clients to spend their money would be a person, board, or organization advising the wealthy on the way to give of their money for the best possible effect on the community.

20. The basic assumption behind social exchange is that people enter into social associations in order to satisfy some want. Rewards of these social associations may be intrinsic, humanitarian and spiritual, as in love or sociability; or extrinsic, such as goods and services sought for personal advantage and emotional satisfaction. Most social associations bring rewards which fall between these two extremes. The whole process of social exchange follows a protocol, as established by the particular culture, although this protocol is entirely informal or unwritten (unlike an economic exchange with its formal contract) – Blau 1974, 204-14. For further details and illustrations from Martial's poems, see Ch. 2; also Spisak 1998.

21. Cf. Gold 2003, 592: 'Quite unlike his Augustan counterparts, who take pains to downplay interest in financial remuneration and stress the importance of poetry over any payment for it (cf., e.g., Prop. 1.6; 3.9), Martial seems almost to flaunt his need for money and to press the point in embarrassingly obvious ways. This has given rise to many condemnations of Martial for being shrill, servile, undignified, bullying and mendicant.' In her note to this passage (n. 6) Gold gives several examples of these types of reactions to Martial's comments on money.

22. Iuv. 7; see also Martial 1.107; 8.55; 11.3; 12.3; 12.36. Saller 1983, 254, however, warns about the danger of generalizing on the issue of patronage.

23. Just the type of profit Martial has in mind for his poetry is defined in the next poem in the book, 5.16: there he tells his reader that his preference for writing entertaining literature, which gives him notoriety, costs him dearly. For, if he chose to practise as a lawyer, he would get gifts and money enough to make him rich.

24. Gold 2003, 603, suggests that Martial, like Simonides, was caught between a gift-giving economy, where wealth was expected to be exchanged freely in the community, and a money economy, where individuals tried to accumulate money and power – cf., for example, epigram 12.53: a condemnation of the very wealthy Paternus who gives nothing away and guards his treasure like a mythical dragon. See further Gold 2003, 598-600, for an explanation of these two antithetical types of economies and their effects on poets. For another side of the issue, however, see Howell 1995, 97 (at intro. to 5.19), who makes an illuminating point concerning Martial's address to the emperor on the issue of lack of remuneration for his poetry: 'Martial often complains about the meanness of patrons (compare Juvenal's seventh Satire), wishing that great patrons like Seneca and Piso could still be found. However, the fate of those two [both implicated in a plot to assassinate Nero, for which they died] provides at least one good reason why distinguished senators might be wary of devoting too much attention to their *clientelae*.' In other words, it was politically dangerous for highly placed persons to gain too much notoriety through their largess because it made them a potential threat to the emperor – cf. Martial 12.3.9-12, where Martial praises Priscus Terentius for being generous to him especially under a harsh emperor (Domitian) and during evil times.

25. Blau 1964, 106: as Blau puts it, the exchange of gifts and services in simple societies 'serves not only to create bonds of friendship and trust between peers but also to produce and fortify status differences between superiors and inferiors.' He then notes that the 'pervasive exchange processes in modern society ... have the same paradoxical twofold implication.' For details on this superordination process see Blau 1964, 106-12.

26. See Verboven 2002, 47-8, on the concept of *dignitas*, 'honour' or 'prestige', based on the power to gives others what they wanted or needed (he quotes Saller 1982, 126 on this), and thus being diminished if a person was unable to reciprocate in the exchange of *beneficia*.

27. On establishing trust and building and maintaining community through social exchange, see Ch. 2.

28. Cf. Garnsey and Saller 1997, 97, on how social status is affected by exchange: 'Because benefaction and requital were matters of honor, the dynamics of the exchange partially determined the relative social standing of the men involved.'

29. Cf. Sullivan 1991, 129-30: '... for Martial, as for other poets including his rival Statius and his friend Juvenal, and indeed the equestrian class as a whole, the imperial system offered most by way of patronage, prestige and the social utilisation of their talents.' See below on the significance of Martial's interaction with Domitian.

30. The three emperors Martial addresses or mentions in his twelve-book collection are Domitian, Nerva, and Trajan; Titus is addressed in the *Liber de Spectaculis*. Poems that only allude to the reigning emperor (e.g. 1.51; 1.60) or which contain only passing mention of him (e.g. 9.11; 9.16) are not included in this count.

31. Epigrams/prose epistles on or to Domitian are: 1.4; 1.5; 1.6; 1.14; 1.22; 1.104; 2.2; 2.91; 2.92; 4.1; 4.3; 4.8; 4.27; 4.30; 5.1; 5.2; 5.3; 5.5; 5.6; 5.7; 5.15; 5.19; 5.65; 6.2; 6.3; 6.4; 6.10; 6.80; 6.83; 6.87; 7.1; 7.2; 7.5; 7.6; 7.7; 7.8; 7.60; 7.61; 7.99; 8 *praef.*; 8.1; 8.2; 8.4; 8.11; 8.15; 8.21; 8.24; 8.26; 8.36; 8.39; 8.49; 8.53; 8.56; 8.65; 8.66; 8.78; 8.80; 8.82; 9.1; 9.3; 9.5; 9.7; 9.18; 9.20; 9.24; 9.31; 9.34; 9.36; 9.39; 9.64; 9.65; 9.79; 9.83; 9.91; 9.93; 9.101. See Leberl 2004, 245-342; Nauta 2002, 335-440; and Lorenz 2002, 111-246, for a discussion of these (consult their indices).

32. On the *ius liberorum* see S. Treggiari, *Roman Marriage* (Oxford 1991), 66-80; on Martial's usage here, see Williams 2004, 277.

33. On the idea of Martial's imperial panegyric as constructed literary accounts see Lorenz 2002, 4-21, and passim.

34. See Nauta 2002, 339-40 on Martial's play on the two senses of *libellus*: a formal petition in prose that was handed to the emperor in person; and

Martial's books of poetry, wherein he could ask the emperor for favours. See Watson and Watson 2003, 105-7, on 2.91 and its follow-up, 2.92, as a poetic version of a formal petition. Moreover, a petition may not have been necessary at all, for Martial tells us (via his poet-persona) at epigrams 3.95.5 and 9.97.5 that he had been granted the right of three children by 'each emperor', which, because of the dating of the poems, could only mean Titus and Domitian; and yet, Dio Cassius (67.2.1) expressly states that Domitian on his accession confirmed all gifts made by his father and brother, which would thus have made Martial's request in epigram 2.91 unnecessary (see D. Daube, 'Martial, Father of Three', *AJAH* 1 (1976): 145-7, for more details). Also see Watson and Watson 2003, 108 for the sense of 2.92 as an ' "anti-wife" joke of the kind found in Comedy and elsewhere in Martial'.

35. See Lorenz 2002, 42-54, 121, on 2.91 and 2.92 as constructed dialogue designed to praise the generosity of Domitian. Martial also jokes with Domitian about the patronage between the two at 1.6, 4.27, and 5.19.

36. See Lendon 1997, 126-9, on emperors engaging in social exchange. For another level of intention and hence purpose to this poem, wherein Martial uses the petition format, see at 8.54 below.

37. Cf. at 4.27.4, where the poet-persona boasts that the emperor has given him gifts that no one else could give.

38. 8.82.5-8 for the quoted parts; on the civic and military crowns see Schöffel 2002, 690-1. For other poems wherein Martial speaks of his exchange with the emperor, cf. 5.6, where Domitian's chamberlain, Parthenius, is asked to present Martial's book to the emperor; 6.10, 6.87, and 7.60, where Domitian is equated with (or outdoes) Jupiter in his capacity to give; and 9.18, where the poet asks Domitian for water-rights for his town house, again likening him to Jupiter. The three poems (besides 2.91 and 2.92) wherein Martial couches his requests for exchange from the emperor as jokes – 1.6, 4.27, and 5.19 – have been noted.

39. On Martial's petitions to the emperor see Schöffel 2002, 239-40.

40. On the topos of likening the emperor to Jupiter see Sauter 1934, 54-78, and Scott 1936, 133-40; cf. Pitcher 1998, 65-72.

41. See Millar 1992, 468-9, on the goodness of the emperor being determined by his accessibility to petitioners and his discriminate responses (as cited by Nauta 2002, 339, n. 47).

42. As noted by Nauta 2002, 387, with n. 32; also, as Nauta observes, *euergetism* was Statius' most frequent theme (in the *Silvae*); also see Nauta 2002, 327-35, on the synonymous 'community patronage'. The term *euergetism* is from the Greek εὐεργετέω, 'do good' (cf. Latin *benefacio*) – see P. Veyne, *Bread and Circuses: Historical Sociology and Political Pluralism* (London 1990), 10ff. for its history and use. Cf. Fronto *Princ. Hist.* 20 (van den Hout): 'The Roman populace is held by two things in particular, grain distributions and spectacles' (cited by Lendon 1997, 123, with n. 79).

43. Nauta 2002, 388; cf. 327-35, where Nauta describes community patronage.

44. Garnsey and Saller 1997, 97-9 (with notes), on the emperor's patronal relationship, as established by Augustus, and its ideology: for ancient sources they cite the *Res Gestae* 15-18; Pliny's *Panegyric* 2 and 21; and Seneca *Clem.* 1.13.5. See also Saller 1982, 73-8; as he (78) sums up his view, 'The most successful emperors were those who, like Augustus, were able to utilize skillfully the offices, honors, statuses and administrative decisions at their disposal to produce cohesion in a web of personal exchange relationships extending from themselves.'

45. For an explanation of basic principles of social exchange theory see Ch. 2.

46. The theory of secondary exchange is from Blau 1974, 212-14.

47. See Wirszubski 1968, 160-7; cf. Earl 1967, 80: 'The restoration of the Republic in the definition of the Republican nobility had long since [i.e. at the end of Tiberius' reign] ceased to be practical policy and rapidly declined into a display of sentimentality or affection.'

48. *Dominus deusque* used of Domitian at 5.8.1, 7.34.8, 8.2.6, and 9.66.3. Martial's lament appears at 10.72.1-3, on which see below. Another example of what appears to be insincere praise is Martial's lauding Domitian's newly built palace at 8.36.1, and then his condemning the extravagance of its furnishings at 12.15.4-5 – as voiced by Jones 1992, 196.

49. Cf. Finley 1983, 34-49, on the idea of 'community patronage' – where a member of the elite of a city offers goods and services to that city in exchange for honour, prestige, and power from the community (cited by Nauta 2002, 328).

50. Suetonius gives as reasons for Domitian's assassination: his executions of senators and courtiers (10-11; cf. Tac. *Agr.* 45.1ff.); his extortion; and his extreme arrogance – oftentimes taking the form of his equating himself to a god.

51. Cf. Jones 1992, 196, on the cause of Domitian's assassination: '... Domitian's fate was determined essentially by his inability to work with his courtiers. His suspicious nature caused him to begin executing members of his personal staff, those closest to him wherever the court was. The outcome was inevitable.'

52. On Domitian's use of the title *dominus deusque* see Suet. *Dom.* 13.2; on Martial's use of it for Domitian see n. 48. Late sources allege Domitian required it; Suetonius and Dio Cassius (67.4.7) do not. For a full discussion see Scott 1936, 102-12; Nauta 2002, 382-3, with notes.

53. Nauta 2002, 382. Nauta cites S.R.F. Price, *Rituals and Power: The Roman Imperial Cult in Asia Minor* (Cambridge 1984), 65-77, for negotiations being part of establishing the imperial cult. The general process is that an individual, city, or provincial council petitioned for the right to establish a divine cult for the emperor through, e.g., the establishing of rites and priests, the erecting of a statue, or the building of a temple to him. The emperor either granted or refused the petition according to political concerns, including the effect his acceptance might have on the Roman aristocracy's opinion of him – see Lendon 1997, 169 with notes specifically on this last point. Also see Lendon 1997, 163 with notes on the imperial cult's basis in reciprocity: 'Cult was offered to the emperor because of the greatness of his honour, and because of his benefactions – in our terms, both from deference and reciprocity.'

54. See Lendon 1997, 168-70, on the sensitivity and significance of the emperor's acceptance and denial of the imperial cult; on the sensitivity of the Romans to the title of *rex* for the emperor see L. Wickert, 'Princeps (civitatis)', *RE* 22 (1954): 2108-18, as cited by Nauta 2002, 170.

55. On this point see Hoffer 1999, 5-6, in his discussion of the panegyric aspect of the letters of Pliny (Martial's contemporary). After observing that Pliny had to work especially hard 'to maintain the fragile distinctions on which government under a "good emperor" depends' (5), Hoffer states: 'The boundary between emperor and senator remained blurry because by a mutually acceptable fiction, the role of emperor scarcely existed. In principle the emperor was merely a high-ranking senator with supplementary powers and honours, including *imperium*, tribunician *potestas*, the position of Pontifex Maximus, control of the imperial wealth, and especially control of the armies and praetorian guard' (6). Thus, as Hoffer goes on to illustrate in his subsequent discussion of Pliny's remarks on Trajan in his letters, defining both the role of the good emperor and that of the good senator was a real art (6-8).

56. See 5.2, 8 *praef.*, and 8.1 where Martial states his intent to cut back on obscenity and sexual content. Martial's deliberate curbing of these in order to accommodate Domitian is especially visible with Book 11 – written after Domitian's assassination, wherein Martial celebrates the freedom he again has under Nerva to throw out the moral code and write as he wishes (see 11.2). On Domitian's programme of moral reform see Suet. *Dom.* 8.3; Jones 1992, 76, 99, 101-2, 106-7.

57. E.g. 8 *praef.* 8, where Martial refers to Domitian's 'celestial modesty' (*caelesti verecundiae*). On Domitian's morality being questionable, at 11.7.1-5 Martial addresses a wanton and adulterous woman who no longer has the excuse for her adultery of being summoned by Domitian to one of his villas; on Domitian's lustful behaviour see Suet. *Dom.* 22; Dio Cass. 67.12.1.

58. On origins and history of imperial panegyric see Coleman 1998, 338; Ramage 1989, 642-55; also Dewar 1994; and Geyssen 1996, 3-16; on early imperial prose panegyric see Braund 1998, with notes; on Martial's use of the common motifs see Sauter 1934. On the modern readers' inherent aversion to imperial panegyric see Dewar 1994, 209: 'The extravagance of the medium, with the high value it placed on sheer outrageousness of idea and expression alike, will always be alien in some measure to the modern reader'; and Geyssen 1996, 1: 'That the "modern reader" is unaccustomed to the type of flattery found in many of the poets of the early Principate is not surprising, nor can a certain amount of aversion to the idea be denied. Indeed, the level of disbelief is increased when an emperor who has been branded a monster by ancient historians is the recipient of excessive or even tasteless praise. The very thought, for instance, that a figure such as Domitian might have been lauded by an artist of integrity is perplexing.'

59. See Ch. 1 for Martial's justification of his poems' obscenity and sexual content. Given the clash between Martial and Domitian on sexual morality, it is not surprising to find that most of the perceived criticism of Domitian that has been attributed to Martial has to do with sexual morality – see Holzberg 1988, 79-85, as noted by Nauta 2002, 432, n. 176. See above, this Chapter, on Garthwaite's interpretation of sections of Books 6 and 9 as a condemnation of Domitian's morality.

60. See Spisak 1994a, 84-6, an analysis of 12.43, Martial's condemnation of a shameless treatment in verse of sexual practices – what would be classified as pornographic today.

61. Cf. Nauta 2002, 419, on the 'two levels' on which sincerity operates: 'at the level of speech act and at the level of content [on this point Nauta cites Dewar 1994, esp. 201-2]. At the level of speech act praise is "sincere" if it is meant as praise, and not at the same time as criticism. But at the level of speech content such praise does not need to be "sincere" in the sense that the author believes in the truth of what he says. Because the effectivity of the praise does not depend on it, "sincerity" at this level is largely a private matter.'

62. See Braund 1998, for panegyric, partly laudatory and partly protreptic, tailored to the subject and the specific situation – specifically, Pliny on Trajan (58-68); Cicero on Julius Caesar (68-71); Seneca on Nero (71-4); and Cicero on Pompey (74-5).

63. See Braund 1998, 62, who posits protreptic – i.e. a prescribing of ideals – as part of imperial panegyric; and for the similar interpretation of Pliny's *Panegyricus* as a manifesto of senatorial prerogatives (as opposed to an act of imperial fawning) see J. Moles, 'The Kingship Orations of Dio Chrysostom', in *Papers of the Leeds International Seminar 6* (1990): 302-3; and for imperial panegyric as a didactic piece meant to serve as a model for the ruler see G. Picone, *L'eloquenza di Plinio: teoria e prassi* (Palermo 1978; also as cited by Bartsch 1994, 274, n. 5).

64. See, e.g., Garthwaite 1990, 1993, 1998.

65. For the latter point, see Coleman 1998, 338, who in her evaluation of the political role of the Martial Book 8 lists as one of her five points: 'Martial intends the book [i.e. Book 8] to make a positive impression on his readership, i.e. the emperor plus all his other actual and potential patrons, fans, purchasers; subversion would taint all the individuals associated with the book.'

66. On the social and religious sanction given the iambist, see Ch. 1. For what it is worth to the sceptic, Martial specifically claims allegiance to this tradition of candidness at his preface to Book 1 by informing his reader that his poems have no subtext: there he warns the malicious interpreter to stay away from the *simplicitas*, the 'singleness' or 'straightforwardness' of his jokes; these jokes must not be rewritten, he says, so that they can be interpreted to mean something else (1 *praef.* 7-9).

67. Note that Phaedrus, who could be included in the iambic tradition for his animal fables, did have a hidden transcript to his writings, although not directed against the emperor; yet, true to the characteristic candidness of the iambic poet, he actually tells the reader that his poems do conceal a political commentary (*Prol.* 3.33ff.), thus maintaining the iambic tradition of candidness.

68. Jones 1992, 196-8, lists as his major strengths his ability to govern by his own standards; his close personal involvement with administration; and the comparative efficiency and justice of the system itself. For his weaknesses, Jones gives 'his preference for his own company and inability to mix widely amongst the aristocracy' (198).

69. Jones 1992, 196-8, the most recent book-length treatment of Domitian, where Jones speaks of the difficulty in assessing the character and reign of Domitian, and in his concluding remarks calls him an enigma (198).

70. Ramage 1989, 646; Ramage's premise is that Nerva, Trajan, and Hadrian did not promote and may have even actively discouraged formal praise of the reigning *princeps* (see 641). He bases this premise primarily on the evidence from Pliny's *Panegyricus* and Martial's *Epigrams* (see 640-64).

71. Nerva was so mild that he prompted comment by his consul, Fronto, as recorded by Dio 68.1.3: Fronto is said to have remarked that it was bad to have an emperor under whom nobody was permitted to do anything, but worse to have one under whom everybody was permitted to do everything (as cited by Jones 1992, 198; see further 194-5).

72. On this tradition of denigration of previous rulers as eulogy of the present ruler see Ramage, 1989, 640-50.

4. The Good Life

1. E.g. J. Bramble from 'Martial and Juvenal', ch. 29 of E.J. Kenney (ed.), *Cambridge History of Classical Literature II, Latin Literature* (Cambridge 1982), 600, characterizes Martial as 'a court jester' who 'never makes us think' and whose poetry is without any 'moral reflection'.

2. 1.15; 1.49; 1.55; 2.59; 2.90; 3.4; 3.38; 3.58; 4.5; 4.54; 4.66; 5.20; 5.58; 5.64; 6.27; 7.47; 8.44; 8.77; 10.30; 10.47; 10.51; 10.58; 10.74; 10.96; 12.18.

3. *Vivo, vivere* in the sense of living life to the fullest: 1.15.12; 1.103.12; 5.20.14; 5.58.1, 7, 8; 6.27.10; 6.70.15; 8.44.1; 8.77.7; 10.38.9; 12.60.6; cf. Seneca *de Brevitate vitae* 7.3; see further at 1.15 in Ch. 3.

4. On *imagines* and their association with high birth and achievement see Williams 2004, 273; also see Shackleton Bailey 1993, 197, n. b: 'Pride of birth is linked with desire for wealth as a distraction from life's enjoyment because it implies ambition.' Cf. Pliny *HN* 35.2.6-8, where he cites the practice of some families of laying false claim to famous men and displaying *imagines* of those with whom no relationship existed (as cited by Earl 1961, 19).

5. Poems using an urban-rural antithesis to present a pastoral ideal: 1.49; 1.55; 2.90; 3.58; 4.66; 5.20; 10.30; 10.47; 10.51; 10.58; 10.96; 12.18. It was a common topic among the ancient Romans – the theme of whether urban or rural life was better was even placed first by Quintilian on his list of debating topics for students (Quint. 2.4.24, as cited by Braund 1989, 23); see Kier 1933 on ancient Greek and Roman praise of the rustic life as opposed to conditions in the city; also MacMullen 1974, 28-56; see Vischer 1965, 154-5, on the Romans; and see Braund 1989 for the treatment of the theme by the Roman satirists. For a fuller treatment of the urban-rural antithesis specifically in Book 10 see Spisak 2002, 132-4.

6. Cf. 8.44, where Martial presents a more elaborate image of an avaricious person who is wasting away his life: the addressee, Titullus, an old man, is advised that he cannot start enjoying his life too soon. For even in his old age Titullus spends all his days performing salutations and tending to business in all three forums so that he might 'snatch, amass, seize, and possess [money]' (9). It will all have to be left behind, anyhow, at his death, Martial says, and will not even be properly appreciated by his heir and family.

7. For hearths as a topos for the simple country life see Watson and Watson 2003, 141 and 148; in Martial *focus* is a regular element of the country life: 1.49.27, 1.55.8, 10.47.4, 10.96.8, 12.18.19. On the wealthy not using their hearths see Post 1908, 75, who says in explanation of *focus*: 'a real hearth in the old-fashioned atrium of M.'s house; this is clear from the allusion to the smoke; because of the fine marbles and paneled ceilings fires on a true hearth were unknown in the atria of the rich.' Also, large, open fires were a great hazard in the city – see Watson and Watson 2003, 148 and 301.

8. Stricture in the sense that the owner does not use his hearth because he fears to damage his property, primarily with the smoke, but also with the fire itself.

9. Cf., e.g., Hor. *Epist.* 1.10.19-25, where in his praise of life in the country he claims grass to be superior to marble floors and water from streams superior to water from lead pipes, and condemns the practice of 'growing trees among showy columns' (22) as not genuine. See Vitruvius 8.6.10-11 on lead pipes producing a bad taste and being injurious to one's health (as cited by Mayer 1994, 184).

10. Cf., e.g., Juv. 11.147-53, where the poet-persona's slaves are described as native to Italy and rustic in their background and manners. On such slave buying as an extravagance, cf. Martial 3.62.1, where, as an example of the addressee's misuse of his wealth, he condemns him because he 'buys boys [i.e. slaves] at a hundred thousand [sesterces] each, often two hundred'.

11. Cf. Juv. 4.34ff., where he elaborates on the dangers of a too learned woman; cf. also Martial 11.19 on a woman who is *diserta*, 'well-spoken' or 'eloquent', making a bad wife.

12. As Howell 1980, 236, notes, requests for land from the wealthy friends or patrons for self-support are common in the literary sources (Howell cites White 1978, 91). Howell further notes that Martial's wish need not be taken as a serious request (he may have already possessed his villa at Nomentum).

13. Examples of complaints about the morning salutation: 1.70.16-18; 3.4.5-6; 5.20.5-7; 8.44.4-5; 9.92.5-6; 10.58.11-12; 10.70.5-6; 11.24; 12.18.4-5.

14. See Howell 1980, 240-1, s.v. *albus*, which Howell glosses as 'without a healthy tan', and notes that it is not complimentary when used of persons; he also gives as support 3.58.24 and 10.12.7f., and mentions 'the notorious unhealthiness of Rome (especially in the summer)'. On the healthfulness of the rural setting see Kier 1933, 58-62.

15. For 'sell empty smoke' Shackleton Bailey 1993, 280, n. d, glosses:

'Proverbial, of making empty promises'. Canus and Glaphyrus are musical artists (Shackleton Bailey 1993, 281, n. d).

16. Philomelus, listed as fictitious by Shackleton Bailey (1993, 374) is depicted as very wealthy at 3.31.6.

17. Cf. 3.38 where Martial informs his addressee, Sextus, a good man (*vir bonus*) who has come to Rome, that the only way for an honest person to survive in the city is 'to live by chance [i.e. from hand to mouth]' (14).

18. Cf., e.g., 9.2, where the addressee, Lupus, is described as a poor man to friendship (*amicitia*) and thus leaves his friends in need, but spends extravagantly on his mistress – i.e. his personal and sexual desires.

19. Cf. Braund 1989, 28, who in looking at the urban-rural antitheses in the Roman satirists draws the following picture of the city: it was dangerous, expensive, crowded, uncomfortable and unhealthy, and especially marked by behaviour that was artificial and pretentious, highly competitive, and unethical and immoral.

20. Cf. Cicero *Rosc. Am.* 20.44.74-5, where he alludes to the idea that the luxury of the city bred malicious crimes; also cf. Braund 1989, 28, on the city-country antithesis in Roman satire: 'All these antitheses add up to an attitude which identifies city life with greed, corruption and selfishness and idealises country life as a haven where a better set of moral values can be found.'

21. Cf., e.g., 10.10, where Martial castigates his addressee, a man of consular rank, who, because he debases himself by cultivating patrons most obsequiously, prevents the poet-persona from securing benefits.

22. On the corrupting and destructive force of greed and lust for power taking hold in the second century BCE see Earl 1967, 17-19; and Earl 1961, 41-4, and 49-51, for a convenient listing of numerous references; also cf. Hor. *Epist.* 1.53-5, where Horace imagines that the cry throughout the forum is money before virtue (*virtus*); Ov. *Met.* 1.127-50; *Ars Am.* 277ff.; Juv. 13.28ff. On the ancient Roman society as 'imbued with the doctrine of acquisition' (56) see Segal 1968, 55-7.

23. Julius Caesar's career is a good example of the difficulty the ancient Romans had with trying to maintain their ambitions at a reasonable and socially productive level: e.g. was Caesar's own notoriously high ambition good or bad for the Roman State? Augustus' career is even more difficult to assess, since he managed to keep his personal ambition in the background while attaining so much wealth and power.

24. Sallust regularly gives *ambitio* a negative sense: 'Yet at first ambition [*ambitio*] more than avarice [*avaritia*] was stirring up the minds of people, which [i.e. *ambitio*], although a vice, was nearer to a virtue. For both the good and the bad person wishes glory, honour, and power for himself; but the former uses the true path, while the latter, who is lacking in good skills, strives for these things using craft and deception' (*Cat.* 11.1-3). In other authors *ambitio* can have its positive sense – e.g. Sherwin-White's summation of Pliny's use of it: 'In Pliny the word *ambitio* has the general sense of currying favour, without any undertone of corruption' (Sherwin-White 1966, 341).

130

25. Sallust's Catiline is a fine example of the lure and dangerous effects of immoderate *ambitio*: Sallust portrays him as incredibly gifted, but evil and depraved by nature, and one whose 'insatiable mind was always desiring that which was immoderate, incredible, and over the top [*nimis alta*]' (*Cat.* 5.1-5). His ambition took tangible and highly dangerous form with his attempted coup.

26. Quintilian's accomplishments: an advocate for twenty years (Quint. *Inst.* 1. *pr.* 1); probably the first rhetorician to receive a salary (under Vespasian, Suet. *Vesp.* 18); unusually wealthy for one in his profession (Juv. 7.186ff.); the teacher of Pliny the Younger (Pliny *Ep.* 2.14.10), as well as the tutor to Domitian's two great-nephews and heirs (Quint. *Inst.* 4. *pr.* 2), and the tutor to the sons of Flavius Clemens, through whom he gained the *ornamenta consularia* (Auson. *Grat. Act.* 7.31) – all as cited by *OCD*, s.v. 'Quintilianus' (R.G. Austin).

27. Societal expectations and the need for public approval were particularly strong for upper class Romans – see, e.g., Earl 1961, 18-27, for a description of what comprised aristocratic *virtus*; on their strong drive to acquire money see D'Arms 1981, 20-2, 152-5.

28. Lovejoy and Boas 1965, 7, define cultural primitivism as a 'discontent of the civilized with civilization, or with some conspicuous and characteristic feature of it'; in its several forms it typically reacts to the complexity of civilized society – the sometimes mindless restrictions and constraints it imposes on the individual, and also the excessive labour it necessitates in order to attain what is considered adequate for a civilized existence (9); they define (7-11) the two major forms of cultural primitivism: 'soft primitivism' (10), where conditions of life are ideal – food in abundance, little or no labour required for survival, harmony among the inhabitants, a long and leisurely existence; and 'hard primitivism' (10), where conditions are hard, but the inhabitants are 'noble savages' and thus able to handle the hardships and make a happy existence. Behind all types of primitivism they posit nature as the norm (11-16), and give numerous citations of primitivistic sentiment found in ancient Greek, Roman, Western Asian and Indian literature (beginning on 23 and continuing throughout the text). For the pastoral theme in ancient literature see Vischer 1965, 126-71; in literature in general, see Daemmrich 1997.

29. As detailed in the above section using epigrams 1.55, 2.90, 4.5, and 5.20.

30. As noted by Post 1908, 251, ad loc., *res* = *res familiaris*, 'money' or 'wealth', a frequent meaning, especially in poetry.

31. As noted by Watson and Watson 2003, 140, ad loc., the comparative degree adjective Martial uses for 'happy life', *vita beatior* – literally, 'happier life' – is not essentially different in sense here from *vita beata*. Perhaps, however, Martial with the comparative degree adds the nuance 'happier (than normal) life'. See Sharples 1996, 82ff., for the basic question of ancient ethics (Plato, Aristotle, Epicureans, and Stoics) as 'what life-style or politics should I adopt?' (83), and 'what sort of life constitutes "happiness" ' (84).

131

32. Cf. Sullivan 1991, 216, on 10.47: 'At first sight, the poem is simply a manifesto of a cultivated Epicurean conformist ... But there is a specifically Roman, indeed equestrian, tincture to this receipt for happiness ...' On Martial's Epicureanism see Adamik 1975.

33. See Post 1908, 252, ad loc., who cites Pl. *Resp.* 330B-C, where 'Socrates declares that those who have inherited their wealth are generally free from the vice of caring too much for it.' Post adds in explanation: 'Excessive regard for wealth keeps one from using it.' Cf. MacMullen 1974, 117, whose description of the spectrum of approbation for the Roman nobility in acquiring wealth reflects a class bias: 'At one end lay the very best thing of all, wealth without a person's having to get it himself, that is, inherited. The active pursuit of it aroused certain misgivings, at least among the topmost nobility. They simply *had* money. Next along the spectrum lay wealth enjoyed in retirement; and verging toward the unrespectable, wealth still in the process of accumulation.'

34. See most conveniently Preuss 1994, 230-3, for Epicurean doctrine on wealth and proper lifestyle; see Adamik 1975, 61-2, for Epicurean doctrine applied specifically to epigram 10.47.

35. See Hopkins 1965, 25: 'the socially approved ways in which an aristocrat could get money were restricted to inheritance, dowry and government office.' See also D'Arms 1981, 6: 'the economic pursuits becoming to a man of *dignitas* were pre-eminently agricultural'; and see 20-71 for acceptable ways in which the upper classes could acquire wealth.

36. Cf., e.g., Pliny *Ep.* 1.9.1-5, where Pliny laments his days in the city wasted in the trivialities of everyday business, especially as compared to his use of leisure time at his villa (spent in reading, writing, and exercising).

37. On the toga see Post 1908, 251 ad loc., 45 at n. 5, 63 at n. 4.

38. For the association of tranquillity and peace with the rural life see Kier 1933, 34-41, for many examples from ancient Greek and Roman authors. For the stress and anxiety associated with the city see, e.g., Martial 1.49.31-6, 1.55.13-14, 10.58.6-10, 10.96.7-12, 12.18 passim.

39. Watson and Watson 2003, 141 ad loc., suggest that *mens quieta* evokes Epicurean ἀταραξία, 'freedom from anxiety'. On Epicurean withdrawal from public life see Preuss 1994, 233-4, wherein the main concern is not to compromise one's security and personal freedom by becoming embroiled in public affairs and politics; but, as noted by Preuss (234), Epicureans were not constrained in principle from taking part in public life, and thus could and did do so to accommodate circumstances or as it suited their individual temperament and preference – cf. Plut. *de Tranq. anim.* 466A = Us. 555, which has Epicurus admitting that those constitutionally unable to resist the glory of public life should enter it as the lesser of two evils (as cited by Rist 1972, 139, n. 1).

40. For Martial's boasts of his world-wide fame see 1.1.1-3; 5.13.2-3; 6.64.25; 8.61.3; 10.9.

41. Cf. again Pliny *Ep.* 1.9, where Pliny, after lamenting the triviality of duties in the city, recommends to his addressee that he take time off from the

'the noise, empty bustle, and futile labours' of the city to give himself to study and leisure at his villa (1.9.7).

42. On *ingenuus* as typical of or befitting a free-born person see *TLL* 7.1.1544, s.v., *caput alterum*. So taken by Shackleton Bailey 1993, 368, n. a, who cites similar usages of *ingenuus* at 3.46.6 and 6.11.6; likewise Watson and Watson 2003, 141, ad loc., who cite in addition Ov. *Tr.* 1.5.71-2.

43. See Kier 1933, 58-62, for numerous references.

44. See Kier 1933, 91-6.

45. Martial uses *simplicitas* with its moral sense of 'guilelessness' at 1.39.4 and 8.73.2 – cf. *OLD* s.v., 4, where one of the definitions given is 'naiveté'; also cf. Schöffel 2002, 612-13. Watson and Watson 2003, 141, ad loc., translate *prudens simplicitas* as 'frankness tempered with discretion' and note that it is an Epicurean practice. The Epicurean use of παρρησία, 'frank speech', was, however, specifically for admonishing and censuring members of their group in order to promote moral development – see Konstan, Clay et al. 1998, 5-8. In other words, the Epicurean sense is too specialized to fit Martial's context. Moreover, the adjective *prudens* would not be apt for the Epicurean sense; rather, 'moderate', 'kind', or even 'just' would be more appropriate, since the tendency in giving frank criticism was to be too harsh, or to be insensitive to the nature and state of the subject (see again Konstan, Clay et al. 1998, 13ff.).

46. See Kier 1933, 67-82, for the association of morality with the country; also see above section at epigram 4.5; and cf. Spisak 2002, 133 for the strong connection between the *vir bonus*, 'good man', and Martial's pastoral ideal in Book 10.

47. For *pares amici* as alike in rank Watson and Watson 2003, 141, ad loc. cite Ov. *Tr.* 3.4.44, where Ovid uses *pares amicitias* to mean friendships with those of one's own rank and class. For *pares amici* as congenial friends Post 1908, 252, ad loc. cites Hor. *Ep.* 1.5.25; cf. *OLD* s.v., 6: 'matched in qualities'.

48. See, e.g., 2.43, 3.60, 6.11. One of Pliny's letters (2.6) provides a telling footnote to this practice: he tells of a dinner party he attended where the host served the best dishes to himself and a select few, and cheap scraps of food to the rest. Also this host served three types of wine to his guests: the best to his friends that were his equal in rank, a lesser quality wine to his so-called 'lesser friends' (*minores amici*), and the lowest quality to the freedmen. Pliny, when asked if he approved of this practice, said he did not, and then, when asked what he did, said: 'I serve the same things to everyone, for I invite them to dinner, not to a social review [*nota*] ... ' (2.6.2-3).

49. E.g. 1.7 (et al.) to L. Arruntius Stella, amateur poet of consular rank – see White 1975, 267-72; Grewing 1997, 176-7. For other high ranking friends of Martial's see Sullivan 1991, 16-21, where Sullivan lists Martial's 'friends and patrons' from senatorial circles in Books 1 and 2; Sullivan's summation of the pattern of these associations, which he terms as 'oddly random': 'Much would depend on congeniality of character, as well as shared literary tastes' (21).

50. On Julius Martialis see 1.15, 1.107, 3.5, 4.64, 5.20, 6.1, 7.17, 9.97, 10.47,

11.80, 12.34; Grewing 1997, 69; *PIR²* I.411; *RE* 10.672-4 (343); also see at 1.15 in Ch. 3.

51. On this secondary sense of *convictus* see *TLL* 4.4.875, s.v., 2.

52. See Nisbet and Hubbard 1970 on Hor. *Carm.* 1.20, who describe the invitation poem as a 'minor category of Hellenistic epigram' (as cited by Howell 1995, 157); also see F. Cairns, *Generic Composition in Greek and Roman Poetry* (Edinburgh 1972), 74-5, who classifies the invitation poem to dinner (*vocatio ad cenam*) as an unofficial form of an epideictic *kletikon*, an official invitation. On dinner invitation poems also see Kay 1985, 180-1; G.W. Williams, *Tradition and Originality in Roman Poetry* (Oxford 1968), 125-6. Martial has three such dinner invitation poems: 5.78, 10.48, and 11.52; cf. Catull. 13; Hor. *Ep.* 1.5; and Juv. 11, all invitation poems, and also cf. Pliny *Ep.* 1.14, also an invitation to dinner.

53. Cf. Pliny *Ep.* 1.15.4, where he tells his potential guest that he can dine on richer food at many houses, but nowhere else 'more merrily, more guilelessly, more incautiously' (*hilarius simplicius incautius*).

54. Cf. Juv. 11.183ff., where he tells his potential dinner guest to leave aside business matters for relaxation; and Hor. *Epist.* 1.5.8-9, where he tells his potential dinner guest: 'Drop trifling hopes and the struggle for wealth and Moschus' case.'

55. For the pressured and constrained atmosphere of the Roman dinner party see D'Arms 1999, 318-19.

56. As D'Arms 1999, 314, puts it: '*Delatores* [informers] were a universally despised breed; Seneca and Tacitus reserve special contempt for them because they maliciously twisted the frankness of dinner talk ... into capital crimes' (D'Arms cites Sen. *de Ben.* 3.26-7 and Tac. *Ann.* 6.5).

57. Cf., e.g., in Martial's depiction of rural life at 1.49.29-30, where the huntsman, who is presumably a slave or a freedman, is invited to dinner with a shout (see Howell 1980, 224, ad loc.); or at 3.58.41, where when the work is done, a 'happy neighbour' is asked over for dinner.

58. 'A table without frills' is Shackleton Bailey's (1993) translation.

59. Traditionally the menu in invitation poems is modest (see Kay 1985, 180-1), and Martial follows suit in his own three dinner invitation poems – 5.78, 10.48, and 11.52 (see Gowers 1993, 220-79, on Roman invitation poems, and 250-67, on Martial's three poems). On the rural ideal in food see Kier 1933, 5-20; cf. Martial 1.55.7-12; 3.58.33-40; 4.66.5-8; 10.48.6-20.

60. Martial's poems on drunkenness: 1.11. 1.26, 1.27, 1.28, 1.87, 2.73, 5.4, 6.78, 6.89, 9.87, 11.82, 12.70.

61. E.g. drinking to forget lost love in sleep – 1.71, 1.106, 8.50; or drinking to enjoy life or celebrate 2.59, 5.64, 6.27, 8.45, 8.77, 9.93, 11.6.

62. A state that is a poetic commonplace – see D. Gerber, 'The Measure of Bacchus', *Mnemosyne* 41 (1988): 39-45, as noted by Watson and Watson 2003, 142 ad loc.

63. Epigram 11.104 – on which see Kay 1985, 276-84, for a very helpful commentary – is a graphic and humorous illustration of this seemingly impossible mix that Martial proposes as his sexual ideal for the happy life. After an almost lurid but highly literary description of the type of passion and sexual accommodation he wishes from his wife, the poet sums up by saying to her: 'If graveness pleases you, you can be a Lucretia all day, but I want a Lais at night' (11.104.21-2). Lucretia was the prime exemplar of feminine virtue for the ancient Romans, whereas Lais was an infamous Greek courtesan – see Livy 1.57f for the story of Lucretia; see Kay 1985, 282 ad loc. on Lais.

64. On virtue as associated with the country see Kier 1933, 75-82; also noted by Watson and Watson 2003, 142 ad loc. On adultery and sexual wantonness in Martial's epigrams see Shackleton Bailey 1993, 334, 'Index of Topics', s.v. 'Adultery' and 'Sexual riff-raff'.

65. Sex is certainly a part of Martial's pastoral ideal – see epigram 4.66.11-12, where the rural landowner and dweller had sex as often as he liked with either his bailiff's wife or one of his tenant farmers' wives; and epigram 12.18.22-5, where the poet-persona in retirement in the country has a huntsman of the type 'you would like to have with you in a secret grove' (22-3), and a smooth-skinned bailiff who asks his master to let him cut his hair – which almost certainly indicates that his present role, besides that of bailiff, is as a passive partner in sex to his master.

66. For untroubled sleep as a feature of Epicureanism see Watson and Watson 2003, 143 ad loc.

67. Martial illustrates this type of anxiety at epigram 9.92, a comparison between the life of a slave and that of his master, where the slave's cheap mat is said to give him carefree sleep (*securos somnos*), while the wealthy master lies sleepless, even though on a feather mattress (9.92.3-4). Cf. Henriksén 1999, 138 ad loc., who cites Hor. *Sat.* 1.1.76-9, where the poet, in criticism of those who over-value money, says of the wealthy man's life: 'Staying awake half-dead with fear, living night and day in fear of villainous thieves, fires, and your slaves, that they'll rob you and run away – do you like this type of life?'

68. Cf. also epigram 10.74, where the poet says that what he wants or craves, in return for his many hours spent as a caller and client, is to be rewarded not with money or land, but only with sleep.

69. See again Kier 1933, 33-41, and especially 35-6 with n. 98 specifically on sleeping in the country.

70. This connection between dissatisfaction with one's self and greed and selfish acquisitiveness is shown well by Horace in *Sat.* 1.1. As he phrases it: 'No one because of his greed is satisfied with himself. Rather everyone commends those pursuing different paths, and wastes away because someone else's goat bears a more distended udder. They do not compare themselves to the greater throng of people poorer than they are, but rather struggle to outdo this one and that one' (*Sat.* 1.1.108-12). See Brown 1993, 98-9 ad loc. on the translation of this passage, and 89-90 on the connection between the two themes of one's habitual discontent with his lot and greed or selfish acquisitiveness in this poem.

71. Cf. again Hor. *Sat.* 1.1, where Horace in speaking of how greed causes people to strive continually to outdo all others says: 'This is why we rarely find anyone who says he's led a happy life, and who, when his time is up, leaves from life content, like a satisfied dinner guest' (*Sat.* 1.1.117-19). Also cf. epigram 10.23, where Martial writes in praise of Antonius, a 'happy man', who, although an old man, is said not to fear death because he has lived a good life.

72. Leach 1974, 31. For a survey treatment of the theme of the golden age in ancient literature see Lovejoy and Boas 1965, 23-102.

73. Hes. *Op.* 109-20 for the account of the golden age; 168-75 for Cronus as ruler over the Islands of the Blest; Hesiod's Heroic Age is an exception to the declining quality of the ages.

74. As Versnel 1993, 151, puts it: the Greeks understand the myth of the golden age from a 'theological or anthropological point of view', while the Romans 'tended to express myth in historical terms'; thus for them the age of Saturn is an historical period.

75. On this merging of the ancient Greek Cronus and Roman Saturn see Versnel 1993, 136-46: he refers to it as the 'Hellenization of Saturn'; and Johnston 1980, 62-89. As for Saturn being an agricultural deity, the Romans believed that Saturn's name was derived from the Latin verb *sero, serere, sevi, satus*, 'to sow' (Festus, *Gloss. Lat.* 186b24; 325a15; Varro *Ling.* 5.64; Macrob. *Sat.* 1.10.20), although this is unlikely because the vowel quantity of the 'a' differs (short in *satus*; long in *Saturnus*). Still, the time of his festival, the Saturnalia on 17 December, marked him as agricultural as did as the accounts of him as the king who introduced agriculture to Italy – see further Versnel 1993, 143; and below.

76. *Aen.* 8.314-27; cf. *Aen.* 7.49; 7.203; *Ecl.* 6.41; *Georg.* 2.173; 2.538. For the association of Saturn and an agricultural golden age in ancient Italy see Johnston 1980, 62-89, who uses various passages from Vergil, as well as other sources, to argue this thesis.

77. Macrob. *Sat.* 1.7.21-5 for the entire account; cf. also 1.10.19-20; other sources that depict Saturn as improving conditions for humans: Festus *Gloss. Lat.* 202; Plut. *Quaest. Rom.* 12 and 42; on Saturn as a culture hero see Versnel 1993, 143.

78. Cf. Tacitus' description of early humankind: 'The most ancient human beings then lived with no evil desire, without shame and crime, and therefore without penalties and compulsion' (*Ann.* 3.26).

79. On the Saturnalia as a return to the golden age of Saturn see epigram 14.1.9-10; Lucian *Sat.* 7; Macr. *Sat.* 1.7.26; and Gatz 1967, 136ff. Cf. Lovejoy and Boas 1965, 65-70.

80. My account of the festival comes from Leary 2001, 4-10, and Versnel 1993, 146-50, both with literary sources conveniently cited (for a more thorough listing of the evidence from literary texts see V. d'Agostino, 'Sugli antichi Saturnalia', *RSC* 17 [1969]: 180-7; and G. Wissowa, *Saturnus*, in W.H. Roscher (ed.), *Ausführliches Lexikon der griechischen und römischen Mythologie* 2.2 [Leipzig 1890-97], 427-44 on 436-40); also from Döpp 1993, 146-8; and Scullard 1981, 205-7.

81. See Ch. 1 for the obscene jokes typical of the Saturnalia.

82. See Versnel 1993, 115-16; see also Scott 1990, 185-6, on this safety-valve theory.

83. See Versnel 1993, 116-17; see also Nauta 1987, 90-5, who, in his investigation of the function of the laughter in the *Apocolocyntosis*, considers the 'steam-valve' (= Versnel's so-called safety-valve) theory, as well as other closely related theories.

84. Versnel 1993, 118-21; for the idea of societies as constructions of reality Versnel cites P.L. Berger and T. Luckman, *The Social Construction of Reality: A Treatise in the Sociology of Knowledge* (New York 1971), 121; for the concepts 'deep legitimacy' and 'other reality', and 'periods of exception' (which follow below), Versnel credits P. Weidkuhn, 'The Quest for Legitimate Rebellion. Towards a Structuralist Theory of Rituals of Reversal', *Religion* 7 (1977): 167-88.

85. Versnel 1993, 119.

86. Versnel 1993, 119, n. 99, cites P.L. Berger and T. Luckman, *The Social Construction of Reality: A Treatise in the Sociology of Knowledge* (New York 1971), 121 for the idea that '[a]ll societies are constructions in the face of chaos'.

87. For the Saturnalia's emphasis on gift-exchange as a dialogue on the ethics of patronage – especially for Martial – see Nauta 2002, 184-9.

88. Cf. Bakhtin's (1984b, 6-8) concept of life during the time of carnival, and especially the Saturnalia, as 'a completely different, nonofficial, extraecclesiastical and extrapolitical aspect of the world, of man, and of human relations; … a second world and a second life outside officialdom' (6); also as having 'a universal spirit', and as 'a special condition of the entire world, of the world's revival and renewal' (7).

89. Leach 1974, 31-2. For the archetype of rebirth Leach cites Jung, *The Archetypes and the Collective Unconscious*, trans. by R.F.C. Hull (New York 1949), 80-1, 130; and M. Bodkin, *Archetypal Patterns in Poetry* (New York 1958), 106-10.

Bibliography

Adamik, T., 1975. 'Martial and the *"Vita Beatior"* ', *AUB (Class)* 3: 55-64.

Adams, J.N., 1982. *The Latin Sexual Vocabulary*. London.

Ahl, F., 1984. 'The Art of Safe Criticism', *AJP* 105: 174-208.

Arthur, M.B., 1994. 'Politics and Pomegranates: An Interpretation of the Homeric *Hymn to Demeter*', in H.P. Foley (ed.), *The Homeric Hymn to Demeter*, 214-42. Princeton, New Jersey. (This article originally appeared in *Arethusa* 10 [1977]: 7-47 under the name of Marilyn A. Katz.)

Bakhtin, M., 1984a. *Problems of Dostoevsky's Poetics* (ed. and trans. by C. Emerson). Minneapolis and Manchester.

———— 1984b. *Rabelais and His World* (trans. by H. Iswolsky; 2nd edn). Bloomington.

Baldry, H.C., 1952. 'Who Invented the Golden Age?', *Classical Quarterly* 2: 83-92.

Bartsch, S., 1994. *Actors in the Audience: Theatricality and Doublespeak from Nero to Hadrian*. Cambridge.

Blau, P.M., 1964. *Exchange and Power in Social Life*. New York.

———— 1974. *On the Nature of Organizations*. Malabar, FL; rpt 1983, New York.

Boyle, A.J. (ed.), 1995a. *Roman Literature and Ideology, Ramus Essays for J.P. Sullivan*. Victoria, Australia.

———— 1995b. 'Martialis Revividus: Evaluating the Unexpected Classic', in Boyle 1995a, 250-69.

Bramble, J.C., 1974. *Persius and the Programmatic Satire*. Cambridge.

Braund, S.H., 1989. 'City and Country in Roman Satire', in S.H. Braund (ed.), *Satire and Society in Ancient Rome*, 23-47. Exeter.

Braund, S.M., 1996. *Juvenal, Satires, Book 1*. Cambridge.

———— 1998. 'Praise and Protreptic in Early Imperial Panegyric', in M. Whitby (ed.), *The Propaganda of Power*, 53-76. Leiden.

Brown, C.G., 1997. 'Iambics', in D.E. Gerber (ed.), *A Companion to the Greek Lyric Poets*, 11-88. New York.

Brown, P.M., 1993. *Horace, Satires I*. Warminster.

Brunt, P.A., 1988. *The Fall of the Roman Republic and Related Essays*. Oxford.

Burnett, A.P., 1983. *Three Archaic Poets: Archilochus, Alcaeus, Sappho*. Cambridge.

Cavarzere, A, A. Aloni, and A. Barchiesi (eds), 2001. *Iambic Ideas: Essays on a Poetic Tradition from Archaic Greece to the Late Roman Empire*. Lanham.

139

Citroni, M., 1968. 'Motivo di polemica letteraria negli epigrammi di Marziale', *Dialoghi di archeologia* 2: 259-301.

—— 1975. *M. Valerii Martialis Epigrammaton Liber 1*. Florence.

—— 1989. 'Marziale e la letteratura per i Saturnali (poetica dell'intrattenimento e cronologia della pubblicazione dei libri)', *ICS* 14: 201-26.

—— 1996. 'Latin Epigram', in Hornblower, S. and A. Spawforth (eds), *The Oxford Classical Dictionary* (3rd edn), 536-9. Oxford.

Clayman, D.L., 1980. *Callimachus' Iambi*. Leiden.

Coleman, K.M., 1998. 'Martial Book 8 and the Politics of AD 93', in F. Cairns and M. Heath (eds), *Papers of the Leeds International Latin Seminar* 10, 337-57. Leeds.

Colton, R.E., 1991. *Juvenal's Use of Martial's Epigrams: A Study of Literary Influence*. Las Palmas.

Daemmrich, I.G., 1997. *Enigmatic Bliss: The Paradise Motif in Literature*. New York.

Damon, C., 1997. *The Mask of the Parasite: A Pathology of Roman Patronage*. Ann Arbor.

Damschen, G. and A. Heil, 2004. *Epigrammaton liber decimus: Text, Übersetzung, Interpretationen*. Frankfurt am Main.

D'Arms, J.H., 1981. *Commerce and Social Standing in Ancient Rome*. Cambridge, Massachusetts and London.

—— 1999 (rpt of 1990 edn). 'The Roman *convivium* and equality', in O. Murray (ed.), *Sympotica: A Symposium on the Symposium*, 308-20. Oxford.

Dewar, M., 1994. 'Laying it on with a Trowel: The Proem to Lucan and Related Texts', *Classical Quarterly* 44(i): 199-211.

Döpp, S., 1993. 'Saturnalien und lateinische Literatur', in S. Döpp (ed.), *Karnevaleske Phänomene in antiken und nachantiken Kulturen und Literaturen*, 145-77. Trier.

Dover, K.J., 1963. 'The Poetry of Archilochus', in J. Pouilloux, et al. (eds), *Archiloque, Sept exposés et discussions*, in *Entretiens sur l'antiquité classique, t. 10*, 181-212. Geneva.

Earl, D.C., 1961. *The Political Thought of Sallust*. Cambridge.

—— 1967. *The Moral and Political Tradition of Rome*. Ithaca, NY.

Elliott, R.C., 1960. *The Power of Satire: Magic, Ritual, Art*. Princeton, NJ.

Ferguson, J., 1963. 'Catullus and Martial', *Proceedings of the African Classical Assoc.* 6: 3-15.

Finley, M.I., 1983. *Politics in the Ancient World*. Cambridge.

—— *The Ancient Economy*, 2nd edn (1st edn 1973). London.

Fowler, D.P., 1995. 'Martial and the Book', in Boyle 1995a, 199-226.

Freudenburg, K., 1993. *The Walking Muse: Horace on the Theory of Satire*. Princeton, NJ.

Freyburger, G., 1986. *Fides. Étude sémantique et religieuse depuis les origines jusqu'à l'époque augustéenne*. Paris.

Gaffney, G.E., 1976. 'Mimic Elements in Martial's *Epigrammaton Libri XII*'. Diss., Nashville, TN.

140

Bibliography

Galán Vioque, G., 2002. *Martial, Book VII: A Commentary*. Leiden.

Garnsey, P. and R. Saller, 1997. 'Patronal Power Relations', in R.A. Horsley (ed.), *Paul and Empire: Religion and Power in Roman Imperial Society*. Harrisburg, PA.

Garthwaite, J., 1990. 'Martial, Book 6, on Domitian's Moral Censorship', *Prudentia* 22: 13-22.

―――― 1993. 'The Panegyrics of Domitian in Martial Book 9', *Ramus* 22: 78-102.

―――― 1998. 'Putting a Price on Praise: Martial's Debate with Domitian in Book 5', in Grewing (ed.) (1998), 157-72.

Gatz, B., 1967. *Weltalter, goldene Zeit und sinnverwandte Vorstellungen*. Hildesheim.

Gentili, B., 1988. *Poetry and Its Public in Ancient Greece: from Homer to the Fifth Century*, trans. by A.T. Cole (orig. published as *Poesia e pubblico nella Grecia antica: da Omero al V secolo* [Rome 1985]). Baltimore, MD.

Gerber, D.E., 1999. *Greek Iambic Poetry from the Seventh to the Fifth centuries BC*. Cambridge and London.

Geyssen, J.W., 1996. *Imperial Panegyric in Statius, A Literary Commentary on Silvae 1.1*. New York.

Gill, C., N. Postlethwaite, and R. Seaford, 1998. *Reciprocity in Ancient Greece*. New York.

Gold, B.K., 2003. '*Accipe Divitias et Vatum Maximus Esto*: Money, Poetry, Mendicancy and Patronage in Martial', in A.J. Boyle and W.J. Dominik (eds), *Flavian Rome: Culture, Image, Text*, 591-612. Leiden.

Gowers, E., 1993. *The Loaded Table: Representations of Food in Roman Literature*. Oxford.

Grewing, F., 1997. *Martial, Buch VI: ein Kommentar*. Göttingen.

―――― (ed.), 1998. *Toto Notus in Orbe: Perspektiven der Martial-Interpretation*. Stuttgart.

―――― 2003. Review of Lorenz 2002. *Göttinger Forum für Altertumswissenschaften* (http://webdoc.sub.gwdg.de/edoc/p/gfa/6-03/grewing2.pdf) 6: 1053-70.

Hands, A.R., 1968. *Charities and Social Aid in Greece and Rome*. New York.

Heath, M., 2002. *Interpreting Classical Texts*. London.

Heilmann, W., 1984. ' "Wenn ich frei sein könnte für ein wirkliches Leben ...". Epikureisches bei Martial', *A&A* 30: 47-61.

―――― 1998. 'Epigramme Martials über Leben und Tod', in Grewing (ed.) (1998), 205-19.

Hellegourc'h, J., 1963. *Le vocabulaire latin des relations et des partis politiques sous la république*. Paris.

Henderson, J., 1991. *The Maculate Muse: Obscene Language in Attic Comedy*, 2nd edn (1st edn 1975, New Haven and London). New York and Oxford.

Henriksén, C., 1998. *Martial, Book IX. A Commentary*, vol. 1. Uppsala.

―――― 1999. *Martial, Book IX. A Commentary*, vol. 2. Uppsala.

Hoffer, S.E., 1999. *The Anxieties of Pliny the Younger*. Atlanta, GA.

Holzberg, N., 1986. 'Neuansatz zu einer Martial-Interpretation', *WJA* N.F. 12: 197-215.

—— 1988. *Martial*. Heidelberg.

—— 2002. *Martial und das antike Epigramm*. Darmstadt.

Hopkins, K., 1965. 'Élite Mobility in the Roman Empire', *Past and Present* 32: 12-26.

Howell, P., 1980. *A Commentary on Book One of the Epigrams of Martial*. London.

—— 1995. *Martial. Epigrams V, Edited with an Introduction, Translation & Commentary*. Warminster.

Iso Echegoyen, J.J. and A. Encuentra Ortega, 2004. *Hominem pagina nostra sapit: Marcial, 1900 años después*. Zaragoza.

Johnston, P.A., 1980. *Vergil's Agricultural Golden Age: A Study of the* Georgics. Leiden.

Jones, B.W., 1992. *The Emperor Domitian*. London and New York.

Kay, N.M., 1985. *Martial, Book XI*. London.

Ker, W.C.A., trans. 1919. *Epigrams, with an English Translation*. London and New York.

Kier, H., 1933. *De laudibus vitae rusticae*. Diss., Marburg.

Konstan, D., 1997. *Friendship in the Classical World*. Cambridge.

—— , D. Clay, C.E. Glad, J.C. Thom, J. Ware, 1998. *Philodemus: On Frank Criticism*. Atlanta, GA.

Koster, S., 1980. *Die Invektive in der griechischen und römischen Literatur*. Meisenheim am Glan.

Kurke, L., 1991. *The Traffic in Praise: Pindar and the Poetics of Social Economy*. Ithaca, NY.

Leach, E.W., 1974. *Vergil's Eclogues: Landscapes of Experience*. Ithaca, NY and London.

Leary, T.J., 1996. *Martial Book XIV: The Apophoreta*. London.

—— 1998. 'Martial's Early Saturnalian Verse', in Grewing (ed.) (1998), 37-47.

—— 2001. *Martial Book XIII: The Xenia*. London.

Leberl, J., 2004. *Domitian und die Dichter: Poesie als Medium der Harrschaftsdarstellung*. Göttingen.

Lendon, J.E., 1997. *Empire of Honour. The Art of Government in the Roman World*. Oxford.

Lorenz, S., 2002. *Erotik und Panegyrik: Martials epigrammatische Kaiser*. Tübingen.

Lovejoy, A.O. and G. Boas, 1965 (rpt of 1935 edn). *Primitivism and Related Ideas in Antiquity*. New York.

MacMullen, R., 1974. *Roman Social Relations: 50 BC to AD 284*. New Haven and London.

Mankin, D., 1995. *Horace: Epodes*. Cambridge.

Mause, M., 1994. *Die Darstellung des Kaisers in der lateinische Panegyrik*. Stuttgart.

Mayer, R., 1994. *Horace Epistles, Book I*. Cambridge.

Mendell, C.W., 1922. 'Martial and the Satiric Epigram', *CP* 17: 1-20.

Bibliography

Michel, J., 1962. *Gratuité en droit romain*. Brussells.

Millar, F., 1977. *The Emperor in the Roman World (31BC-AD 337)*, 1st edn (2nd edn 1992, London). Ithaca, NY.

Miller, P.A., 1994. *Lyric Texts and Lyric Consciousness: The Birth of a Genre from Archaic Greece to Augustan Rome*. London and New York.

Miralles, C. and J. Pòrtulas, 1983. *Archilochus and the Iambic Poetry*. Rome.

Muth, R., 1976. 'Martials Spiel mit dem ludus poeticus'. In A.M. Davies and W. Meid (eds), *Studies in Greek, Italic, and Indo-European Linguistics Offered to Leonard R. Palmer*. Innsbruck.

Nagy, G., 1976. '*Iambos:* Typologies of Invective and Praise', *Arethusa* 9.2: 191-205.

―――― 1979. *The Best of the Achaeans: Concepts of the Hero in Archaic Greek Poetry*. Baltimore and London.

―――― 1989. 'Early Greek Views of Poets and Poetry', in G.A. Kennedy (ed.), *The Cambridge History of Literary Criticism*, vol. 1, *Classical Criticism*. Cambridge.

Nauta, R.R., 1987. 'Seneca's *Apocolocyntosis* as Saturnalian Literature', *Mnemosyne* 40: 69-96.

―――― 2002. *Poetry for Patrons: Literary Communication in the Age of Domitian*. Leiden.

Newlands, C.E., 2002. *Statius' Silvae and the Poetics of Empire*. Cambridge.

Newman, J.K., 1990. *Roman Catullus and the Modification of the Alexandrian Sensibility*. Hildesheim.

Nisbet, R.G.M. and M. Hubbard, 1970. *A Commentary on Horace: Odes, Book I*. Oxford.

Obermayer, H.P., 1998. *Martial und der Diskurs über männliche 'Homosexualität' in der Literatur der frühen Kaiserzeit*. Tübingen.

O'Connor, E.M., 1989. *Symbolum Salacitatis, A Study of the God Priapus as a Literary Character*. Frankfurt am Main.

OCD = *Oxford Classical Dictionary*, 3rd edn 1996 (1st edn 1949). (Eds) N.G.L. Hammond and H.H. Scullard. Oxford.

OLD = *Oxford Latin Dictionary*, 1996 (rpt of 1982 edn). (Ed.) P.G.W. Glare. Oxford.

Olender, M., 1990. 'Aspects of Baubo: Ancient Texts and Contexts', in D.M. Halperin, J.J. Winkler and F.I. Zeitlin (eds), *Before Sexuality: The Construction of the Erotic Experience in the Ancient World*, 83-113. Princeton.

PIR² = *Prosopographia Imperii Romani saec. I. II. III*, 1933. Berolini and Lipsiae.

Pitcher, R.A., 1998. 'Martial's Debt to Ovid', in Grewing (ed.) (1998), 59-76.

Post, E., 1908; rpt 1967. *Selected Epigrams of Martial*. New York.

Preuss, P., 1994. *Epicurean Ethics: Katastematic Hedonism*. New York and Ontario.

Putnam, Robert D., 2000. *Bowling Alone: The Collapse and Revival of American Community*. New York.

Ramage, E.S., 1989. 'Juvenal and the Establishment. Denigration of

Predecessor in the "Satires"', in W. Haase (ed.), *ANRW* II 33.1, 640-707. Berlin.

RE = *Real-Encyclopädie der klassichen Altertumwissenschaft*, 1893/1978. Stuttgart.

Reckford, K., 1987. *Aristophanes Old-and-New Comedy*. Chapel Hill and London.

Richardson, N.J., 1974. *The Homeric Hymn to Demeter*. Oxford.

Richlin, A., 1992. *The Garden of Priapus: Sexuality and Aggression in Roman Humor*, 2nd edn (1st edn 1983, New Haven). New York.

Rist, J.M., 1972. *Epicurus, an Introduction*. Cambridge.

Rosen, R.M., 1988. *Old Comedy and the Iambographic Tradition*. Atlanta, GA.

Saller, R.P., 1982. *Personal Patronage under the Early Empire*. Cambridge.

—— 1983. 'Martial on Patronage and Literature', *CQ* 33: 246-57.

Sauter, F., 1934. *Der römische Kaiserkult bei Martial uud Statius*. Stuttgart and Berlin.

Scherf, J., 2001. *Untersuchungen zur Buchgestaltung Martials*. München and Leipzig.

Schöffel, C., 2002. *Martial, Buch 8: Einleitung, Text, Übersetzung, Kommentar*. Stuttgart.

Scott, J.C., 1990. *Domination and the Arts of Resistance: Hidden Transcripts*. New Haven.

Scott, K., 1936. *The Imperial Cult under the Flavians*. Stuttgart and Berlin.

Scullard, H.H., 1981. *Festivals and Ceremonies of the Roman Republic*. Ithaca, NY.

Segal, E., 1968. *Roman Laughter: The Comedy of Plautus*. Cambridge.

—— 2001. *The Death of Comedy*. Cambridge.

Shackleton Bailey, D.R., 1990. *M. Valerii Martialis Epigrammata*. Stuttgart.

—— 1993. *Martial: Epigrams*. Cambridge.

Sharples, R.W., 1996. *Stoics, Epicureans and Sceptics: An Introduction to Hellenistic Philosophy*. London and New York.

Sherwin-White, A.N., 1966. *The Letters of Pliny*. Oxford.

Spisak, A., 1992. *Terms of Literary Comment in the Epigrams of Martial*. Diss. Loyola University of Chicago, Chicago.

—— 1994a. 'Martial's *Theatrum* of Power Pornography', *Syllecta Classica* 6: 79-89.

—— 1994b. 'Martial 6.61: Callimachean Poetics Revalued', *TAPA* 124: 291-308.

—— 1997. 'Martial's Special Relation with his Reader', Collection Latomus, vol. 239: *Studies in Latin Literature and Roman History VIII*, 352-63. Brussells.

—— 1998. 'Gift-giving in Martial', in Grewing (ed.) (1998), 243-55.

—— 1999. 'Martial on Domitian: A Socio-Anthropological Perspective', *The Classical Bulletin* 75.1: 69-83.

—— 2002. 'The Pastoral Ideal in Martial, Book 10', *Classical World* 95.2: 127-41.

144

Bibliography

Steinrück, M., 2000. *Iambos: Studien zum Publikum einer Gattung in der frühgriechischen Literatur*. Hildesheim.

Stephenson, H.M., 1880. *Selected Epigrams of Martial*. London.

Sullivan, J.P., 1977. 'Martial's *Apologia pro opere suo*', in Filologia e forme letterarie, Studi offerti a Francesco della Corte IV, 31-42. Urbino.

—— 1987. 'Martial's Satiric Epigrams', in M. Whitby, P. Hardy and M. Whitby (eds), *Homo Viator; Classical Essays for John Bramble*, 259-65. Illinois.

—— 1991. *Martial: The Unexpected Classic, A Literary and Historical Study*. Cambridge.

—— (ed.), 1993. *Martial*. New York and London.

Swann, B.W., 1994. *Martial's Catullus: the Reception of an Epigrammatic Rival*. Hildesheim.

Szelest, H., 1986. 'Martial – eigentlicher Schöpfer und hervorragendster Vertreter des römischen Epigramms', *ANRW* II 32.4: 2563-623.

TLL = *Thesuarus linguae Latinae*, 1900-. Leipzig.

Verboven, K., 2002. *The Economy of Friends. Economic Aspects of Amicitia and Patronage in the Late Republic*. Brussells.

Versnel, H.S., 1993. *Inconsistencies in Greek and Roman Religion II: Transition and Reversal in Myth and Ritual*. Leiden, New York and Cologne.

Vischer, R., 1965. *Das einfache Leben: Wort- und motivgeschichtliche Untersuchungen zu einem Wertbegriff der antiken Literatur*. Göttingen.

Ward, D., 1973. 'On the Poets and Poetry of the Indo-Europeans', *The Journal of Indo-European Studies* 1: 127-44.

Watson, L., 1998. 'Martial 8.21, Literary *Lusus*, and Imperial Panegyric'. In F. Cairns and M. Heath (eds), *Papers of the Leeds International Latin Seminar* 10, 359-72. Leeds.

Watson, L. and P.A. Watson, 2003. *Martial: Select Epigrams*. Cambridge.

West, M.L., 1974. *Studies in Greek Elegy and Iambus*. Berlin.

White, P., 1975. 'The Friends of Martial, Statius and Pliny, and the Dispersal of Patronage', *HSCPh* 79: 265-300.

—— 1978. '*Amicitia* and the Profession of Poetry', *JRS* 68: 74-92.

—— 1982. 'Positions for Poets in Early Imperial Rome', in B.K. Gold (ed.), *Literary and Artistic Patronage under the Early Empire*, 50-66. Austin, Texas.

—— 1993. *Promised Verse; Poets in the Society of Augustan Rome*. Cambridge.

Williams, C.A., 2002. '*Sit nequior omnibus libellis*; Text, Poet, Reader in the Epigrams of Martial', *Philologus* 146: 150-71.

—— 2004. *Martial* Epigrams. *Book Two*. Oxford and New York.

Wirszubski, C., 1968. *Libertas as a Political Idea at Rome during the Late Republic and Early Principate*. London and New York.

Woodbury, L., 1968. 'Pindar and the Mercenary Muse: *Isthm.* 2.1-13', *TAPA* 99: 527-42.

Wray, D.L., 1996. *Catullus: Sexual Personae and Invective Tradition*. Cambridge.

145

Index

147

151